John Kirkwood Leys

The Lindsays

Vol. III

John Kirkwood Leys

The Lindsays
Vol. III

ISBN/EAN: 9783337051785

Printed in Europe, USA, Canada, Australia, Japan

Cover: Foto ©ninafisch / pixelio.de

More available books at **www.hansebooks.com**

A Romance of Scottish Life

BY

JOHN K. LEYS

IN THREE VOLUMES
VOL. III.

London
CHATTO & WINDUS, PICCADILLY
1888

[The right of translation is reserved]

CONTENTS OF VOL. III.

CHAPTER		PAGE
XXVII.	TWO CONVERSATIONS	1
XXVIII.	TROUBLE DRAWS NEAR	23
XXIX.	AT THE POLICE COURT	39
XXX.	ALEC'S FRIENDS VISIT HIM	61
XXXI.	MISGIVINGS	77
XXXII.	BEFORE THE TRIAL	93
XXXIII.	THE TRIAL	107
XXXIV.	AFTER THE TRIAL	150
XXXV.	MISS MEREDITH INSISTS ON BEING OBEYED	176
XXXVI.	SICK UNTO DEATH	192
XXXVII.	THE FUGITIVE'S RETURN	211
XXXVIII.	TWO YEARS AFTER	229

THE LINDSAYS.

CHAPTER XXVII.

TWO CONVERSATIONS.

Mr. Hatchett drove back to his office in a brown study. When he arrived there he sent for Mr. Beattie, who speedily made his appearance.

'Mr. Lindsay is not here, is he?' were the solicitor's first words.

'No, sir. He has been confined to the house with a bad cold for more than a week.'

'Just fetch me the draft of his uncle's will, if you please.'

Mr. Beattie left the room and came back after a few minutes, saying that he could not find it. This was not surprising, seeing that the document was at that moment reposing in a drawer of Mr. Beattie's writing-table, at his own lodgings.

'You can't find it!' exclaimed Mr. Hatchett, his face becoming more grave.

'No. It is not among the other drafts, nor in any of the drawers of Mr. Lindsay's table. One of them is locked, however, and he has the key. Very probably he has put it there for safety.'

'Likely enough. Did you see the draft before it was sent out?'

'I don't think I did,' said Mr. Beattie, after considering a moment. 'No; I am almost sure I did not. I was very busy at the time; but I remember telling Mr. Lindsay to lay the draft on my table, and I would revise it.'

'Did he do so?'

'I can't say; but I never saw it there, and so the thing escaped my memory.'

'You ought not to have allowed an important draft like that to leave the office, without either settling it yourself or sending it to counsel,' said Mr. Hatchett severely.

'You are quite right, sir. But I was kept in the Master's room till late in the afternoon on the day the will was drawn; and when I came back the draft had gone.'

'Then you should have taken care to go over it the next morning, when it came back.'

'If I had not been so very much occupied, no doubt it would have occurred to me. But the letter Mr. Lindsay wrote to us, particularly desiring that his nephew should prepare his will——'

'I don't forget the letter; but it does not release us from all responsibility,' interrupted the solicitor.

'Has anything happened?' asked the other.

'Well, I should not be surprised if something does happen. It seems that the old gentleman altered an intention he had of leaving an enormous sum of money to the Scotch Presbyterians, and left them only five thousand pounds instead.'

'Rather a sensible thing to do, I should say,' observed Mr. Beattie, with a smile.

'Yes; but the odd thing is that one of the Presbyterian parsons, a Scotchman called Mackenzie, I think, says that he saw the draft' (Mr. Beattie gave a hardly perceptible start), 'and that in it the bequest was five hundred thousand pounds.'

'Then the old gentleman changed his mind later in the day, I suppose,' put in the clerk.

'And stranger still,' pursued the solicitor, 'this man says that he was present when the will was signed, that young Lindsay read it aloud before it was signed, and that he read the bequest "five hundred thousand."'

'Really! That is very odd!'

'Very odd indeed.'

'Was anyone else present?'

'Yes, another nephew. And *he* says that Lindsay read "five thousand pounds" only.'

'It is impossible that Lindsay should have committed a fraud. 'I won't believe it of him for a moment!' exclaimed the managing clerk warmly.

'This nephew's evidence is not disinterested, however,' pursued Mr. Hatchett. 'He shares the residue with young Lindsay; and it must be a very large sum, about half a million, I suppose.'

'Had the minister any interest in it, one way or the other?' asked Beattie.

'No; of course not. His name was in the will, though, as secretary to the trust, or something. Here it is,' he added, unfolding the will as he spoke—'at such a remuneration as the trustees in their discretion may decide.'

'Then the minister's evidence is *not* quite disinterested, any more than that of the other nephew?' remarked Beattie.

'No; but of course there is a vast difference between a few hundreds a year and a quarter of a million. And it seems odd that there should be all these elaborate directions about a secretary, and so on, if the bequest was meant to be only five thousand pounds.'

'Perhaps the direction to change the amount came after the will was drawn, and young Lindsay allowed all the rest of it to remain,' suggested Beattie. 'I should think it quite possible,' continued he, 'that the old man was under this minister's influence, afraid of him, in fact, and that he privately told his nephew to make the sum only five thousand, but to read the will as if it were five hundred thousand, to save himself from having a scene with the minister.'

'Rather a far-fetched explanation,' said Mr.

Hatchett, with a smile. 'Besides, the other nephew, Semple, says that his cousin read "five thousand."'

'One of the two is clearly mistaken,' said Beattie.

'Or lying,' said the lawyer. 'Of course the case on the other side is that the two nephews made up a plan to get this money for themselves. Young Lindsay was to get his uncle to intrust the drawing of the will to him, alter the draft by striking out the word "hundred," and deceive the old gentleman by reading the will as if it had been left in, while the other cousin swears that he read it quite correctly. The minister means mischief; I could see that. Well; we can't say anything about it till Lindsay is convalescent. When do you think I could see him?'

'I expect he will be here to-morrow morning. There was a note from him a day or two ago to that effect.'

'Very good; tell me as soon as he comes.'

And here the conversation ended.

As soon as Mr. Beattie was released from the office that evening he went to Alec's rooms. The invalid was sitting alone, with a large fire to keep him company.

'Well, Lindsay, I congratulate you.'

'On being indoors this dismal weather? I meant to have gone to my uncle's funeral to-day, but the doctor bullied me into giving up the idea.'

'Why didn't you tell me you were going to come in for half your uncle's money?'

'Because I have done nothing of the kind.'

'But you have; and I congratulate you with all my heart.'

'Nonsense. I get five thousand pounds. So does Semple. The bulk of it goes to the Free Church.'

'That was your uncle's original idea, I know; I took his instructions myself to that effect. But you must know very well that he changed his mind, and told you to make his legacy to the Free Kirk five thousand—and quite enough too.'

'I never——' began Alec, bewildered by what he heard.

'Stop a minute, man, and let me speak. I have just seen Mr. Hatchett. He read the will to them all after the funeral, and it seems there was a fine row. As it stands, the legacy to the Kirk is only five thousand pounds.'

'Five *hundred* thousand, you mean.'

'Five *thousand* only, I tell you. I saw the will myself in Mr. Hatchett's hands, when he came back to the office.'

'But this is incredible. I——'

'But I tell you I saw it. And you can see it for yourself, as soon as you are well enough to drive down to the office. Your uncle must have changed his mind, and told you to make it five thousand, and your illness has made you forget it—though I warn you, old man, you had better not say you had forgotten such a thing as that. No one would believe you.'

'There's no forgetting in the matter,' cried Alec, striking the elbow of his chair with his fist. 'My uncle never changed his mind. And what I put in the will was five hundred thousand pounds to trustees for the Free Church.'

'Look here, Lindsay, I'll forget what you have said just now. You did not say it.'

'What on earth do you mean ?'

'Because the time may come when—your memory may serve you better. You *must* remember the fresh instructions.'

'How can I remember instructions that never were given ?'

'They were given, sure enough, and you have forgotten them.'

'They were never given!' shouted Alec, losing his temper.

'You are very dense,' said Beattie, with something like a sneer, throwing himself back on his seat.

'True; I don't understand you,' said Alec haughtily.

Beattie made no reply.

'As you choose, Lindsay,' he said at length. 'But I may point out to you, as a friend, that if your uncle did not tell you to alter the will you are in a very unfortunate position.'

'What do you mean?'

'Don't you see? You are intrusted with the making of a will. (It would have been better if you had refused point-blank to have anything to do with it; but we can't help that now.) And you leave out one little word, the effect of which is that you add a quarter of a million sterling to your own share. Who will believe that that was done by inadvertence? Your uncle *must* have told you himself to let the Free Church bequest be five thousand pounds. Think, now.'

'And to avoid the consequences of my blunder—if I did commit a blunder—I am to invent and swear to a lie,' said Alec, slowly rising to his feet. 'I ought to kick you downstairs; and I would, if I were not as weak as a cat just now. Leave the room, sir.'

'Lindsay, you mistake me altogether,' said Beattie earnestly, also rising to his feet. 'I never meant that you should invent what never happened.'

'It sounded precious like it.'

'If you are certain your uncle gave you no further instructions——'

'I told you before, he never did,' interrupted Alec.

'Then you have made a very nasty blunder, that's all; and one that I am afraid will cost you dear.'

'I don't believe I did. Wasn't it five hundred thousand in the draft?'

'I never saw the draft.'

'Why, I left it on your table to be settled, as you told me to do.'

'I dare say you did; but I have no remembrance of seeing it. Let me think.—That afternoon I was in the Master's chambers till very late, and I was so fagged out that I went and had some dinner before I went back to the office. So, very likely, you sent off the draft thinking I had seen it, when I had not.'

'But haven't you looked for it since, this afternoon, to see what it says?'

'I did look for it, but I couldn't find it.'

'Couldn't find it!' exclaimed Alec, who was getting terribly excited. 'Did you look in my drawers?'

'I looked everywhere,' said Beattie; 'but one of your drawers was locked. Perhaps you put it there.'

'I may have done so, though I don't remember it,' said Alec. 'Unfortunately MacGowan, who engrossed it, has gone. It was his blunder, no doubt; but I ought to have noticed it, of course, for I examined it with him.'

'It is clear that it was in your mind that the legacy had been reduced,' said Beattie; 'for when you read over the will to your uncle you read it "five thousand pounds."'

'I did not!' shouted Alec, starting to his feet a second time. 'Who says so?'

'Your cousin, James Semple, says so.'

'Then he says what is not true!'

'That is very unlikely. But Dr. Mackenzie, who was in the room, declares that you read it "five hundred thousand."'

'And he speaks the truth!'

'Do take care what you say, my dear fellow,' said Beattie, after a pause. 'This is sure to come into the courts in some shape or other. Your cousin will swear to hearing you read "five thousand"—at least, so Mr. Hatchett tells us. How dreadful for you to accuse him of wilful and corrupt perjury! What I believe really happened was this: MacGowan made a mistake in copying the will, and you unfortunately allowed it to pass when you examined it. Then, when you read it, you read mechanically what was before your eyes. You are often a little absent-minded, you know, Lindsay,' he added with a smile.

'I suppose it must have been so,' said Alec at length. 'It is the only way of accounting for it. But Dr. Mackenzie says I read it as if it ran "five *hundred* thousand."'

'Pooh, my dear Lindsay, he heard what he wished and expected to hear. Listen to me. Do you think it likely that if your cousin had heard that after being his uncle's right-hand man all these years he was to have only a share of the residue, worth about ten thousand pounds, he would have submitted without saying a word?'

'No; it is not likely,' said Alec thoughtfully; 'and yet I can't help thinking that it was "five hundred thousand" in the will, and that I read it so.'

'My dear fellow, I do want to impress this upon you—don't be as frank with everyone as you are with me. It might be your ruin.'

'How? What do you mean?'

'This Dr. Mackenzie—what sort of a man is he?'

'He is an arrogant, narrow-minded old ass.'

'Is he the sort of man who would prosecute anyone who had done him an injury?'

'The very man, I should say.'

'Then I think you are in very considerable danger.'

'Danger? Of what? Of course I won't

touch a penny of this money, for I know my uncle meant the Free Church to have it.'

'But your cousin doesn't know it. He may not be so ready to give up so large a sum.'

'Does he say so? Have you seen him?'

'Not I. I haven't seen him for ever so long. But he may not be willing to give up his legal rights; and if this Dr. Mackenzie and his friends should make up their minds to prosecute you criminally——'

'What!'

The shout silenced Beattie. The two men sat looking steadily at each other.

'Lindsay,' said Beattie at length, 'is it not better that you should hear the truth from a friend's lips, rather than from an enemy's? Look at the facts. You made an ugly blunder, by which you stand to make a large profit. Giving up the money will only be taken as a confession of guilt. It cannot save you.'

'I know you are innocent of any wrong intention, my dear fellow,' said Beattie warmly, after a short pause. 'Do you suppose I would take all this trouble if I did not know it? But if you had been as long in the profession as I have been, you would understand how the most innocent man, if he has got into a hole (as you have done), may damage his cause by admissions—that is, by speaking frankly to his enemies. They take your words, and twist them into a confession of guilt. Don't give them the chance of doing that. When Mr. Hatchett questions you, as he is sure to do, tell *him* the truth frankly—say you made a blunder which you cannot account for, that your uncle *may* have changed his mind, but he said nothing of it to you—you're sure of that, by the way?'

'Quite sure.'

'Well, say so frankly. And say you cannot remember reading the very words, but you have no doubt you read the words that were before you in the will. That is true enough, I suppose?'

'Certainly. And yet I could have sworn it was "five hundred thousand."'

'Then you would have followed up one mistake by another, you see. That is only your opinion. The will speaks for itself.'

'I *cannot* understand it.'

'But if Dr. Mackenzie, or any stranger, comes to ask you questions, say not one word —not one word, as you value your reputation. Refer them to me, or to Mr. Hatchett. Say nothing to anybody, either of what you thought were your uncle's intentions, or anything else. It is your only safe course. If the danger passes by, well and good. If it comes to your door, I am ready to stand by you. Can I say more?'

'No. You are very good, Beattie,' said Alec half absently. 'If I have need of anyone to defend me, I am sure the case could not be in better hands than yours.'

'Thank you, Lindsay. Well, if I am to help you, I am entitled to ask you to hold your tongue in presence of the enemy, am I not? It's not what you might say that I am afraid of. It's the construction they might put upon it.'

'Yes; I will follow your advice, Beattie.'

'That's right. You won't repent doing so, I am sure. It's the only sensible thing to do. And now, I see you are very tired and worried, so I'll say good-night.'

*   *   *   *   *

'What a Quixotic fellow!' said Beattie to himself, as he sat in his own room half an hour later, and opened a certain drawer in his writing-table. 'To give up two hundred and fifty thousand pounds for a mere freak! I suppose if his uncle's will had said that the money was to have been thrown into the sea he would have thought it his duty to do it. That was practically what the old man wanted to do. If only the young fool would have taken my hint, and said his uncle told him he had changed his mind, and he was to make the Free Kirk bequest five thousand only, we should have been perfectly safe, with, perhaps, the help of a neat imitation of the old man's initials on the alteration in the draft.

'But he wouldn't rise to it. Some men are like that. Curious. Well; I very much fear our friend may suffer for it. I'm very sorry; but, after all, he has only his own obstinacy to thank for it.'

'I may as well get rid of this,' he continued, taking the draft in his hands. 'No use producing it in court altered, if the prisoner persists that he never was told to alter it, and never did alter it. That seems tolerably plain. If I thought he might change his mind——'

Beattie was holding one corner of the document with his left hand, and the other with his right, and he paused an instant.

'No; no chance of that, what he says he will stick to; I am certain of it.'

And at this point in his soliloquy, Mr. Beattie tore the draft in two, and quietly burned it to ashes.

CHAPTER XXVIII.

TROUBLE DRAWS NEAR.

It may easily be believed that Alec Lindsay passed a sleepless night after his visitor left him. In the early morning he sent for a cab, and drove through a choking fog to Theobald's Road.

An old woman, sweeping out the rooms and lighting the fires, was the only person in the office. Alec ran to his own room, and with feverish haste began opening drawers, and tossing about their contents, turning over bundles of old drafts, and peering behind the rows of books on the bookshelves. The draft he sought for was nowhere to be found. Then he began a more systematic search, going carefully over the whole ground again. Of course it was all in vain.

By this time the clerks had begun to arrive. He went downstairs, searched the desk which had formerly been occupied by MacGowan, and closely questioned all the clerks, only to learn that none of them had seen the paper he was seeking.

Once more he went up to his own room, and threw himself into his chair, completely exhausted. A fit of coughing seized him, and when that passed away, he began to cross-examine his memory for the fiftieth time. Where had he put the draft? He believed he had followed the usual course, and placed it with the other drafts of wills, which, as it happened, were kept in this room. What could have become of it? It was possible that MacGowan had inadvertently carried it downstairs with him, and that it had been left there. Or it was possible that it had fallen from the edge of his table into the waste-paper basket. He questioned the office-keeper. She did not remember seeing any paper such as he described in the waste-paper basket. It might have been there; she could not say after so many weeks. If it was in the basket, no doubt she had used it to light the fires with. She could not, in fact, say anything about it.'

He was still speaking to the woman, when he received a message to the effect that Mr. Hatchett, who had just arrived, wished to see him.

Alec went at once to his employer's room. He was the first to speak.

'Will you be kind enough, sir, to show me my uncle's will?'

'Certainly,' said the lawyer, after a short pause.

He unlocked the safe, and produced the will. With trembling hands Alec Lindsay opened it. There were the signatures, one of them slightly blotted. He remembered them well. And in another moment his eyes were riveted on the fatal words, 'the sum of five thousand pounds.' Again he scrutinized the signatures. Yes; they were undoubtedly genuine. This was the paper his uncle had signed.

Alec folded up the document, and gave it back to Mr. Hatchett.

'I have made a terrible blunder, sir,' he said, in a choking voice. Then, steadying himself, he went on: 'That bequest to the Free Church of Scotland should have been five *hundred* thousand pounds. I cannot understand how it happened.'

'You examined the will with the draft, did you not?' asked the lawyer.

'I did. The fault is mine. But where is the draft, Mr. Hatchett?'

'That was just what I was going to ask

you, Mr. Lindsay,' said the solicitor, with a faint but peculiar smile.

'I have not got it.'

'And I have never seen it. Where did you put it?'

'With the other drafts, I imagine. But I can't swear to that. It may have dropped off my table into the waste-paper basket.'

'Yes,' said the solicitor, in a doubtful tone.

'Sir, you don't suppose that I made away with it?' cried Alec hotly.

'No —— Oh dear me, no! But it is very unfortunate.'

This was exactly what the lawyer did believe, however. He might have thought it possible that the omission of the word 'hundred' had been a blunder—but for the disappearance of the draft.

Neither spoke for a few moments. Mr. Hatchett thought it better, considering that his clerk might be charged with a criminal offence, to ask him no more questions, but leave him to frame his defence as he thought best. He believed the young man had yielded to sudden temptation, and had repented of it after destroying the tell-tale draft.

'You are not looking at all well, Mr. Lindsay,' he said, in a not unkindly tone. 'Indeed, you ought not to be out at all on such a day as this. Let me advise you to go home, and try to dismiss the subject from your mind.'

Alec followed the former part of his advice; to follow the latter part of it was impossible. The subject haunted him. To be alone with it was unendurable; he must take counsel with someone; and his thoughts naturally turned to Hubert Blake.

In the afternoon he went to Blake's studio, but it was empty. So Alec told the cabman to drive to Highgate.

It was nearly dark when he arrived there,

and afternoon tea was laid in the drawing-room. Blake was there, and Sophy Meredith, and an elderly lady whom Alec did not know. This was a Miss Elmwood, who had been installed as Sophy's companion.

The atmosphere of peace, of comfort, of freedom from everything like care or anxiety, was inexpressibly soothing to Alec. His friends welcomed him warmly, though Sophy gently reproached him, and Blake roundly told him he was a fool, for venturing out of doors when he was so ill.

'I have something to say to you, Blake,' he said, as soon as he could get an opportunity of speaking aside to his friend. 'I have got into a most horrible mess, and I want your advice.'

Blake's face became serious in a moment.

'You know I am entirely at your service, Alec. If I had known you were so ill, I would have been with you. I can't ask you to come upstairs, for there is no fire there, and the one in the library is very low. But in a minute or two Miss Elmwood will go to sit with my uncle; she always does so at this hour; and I will tell Miss Meredith that we want to be left alone.'

'Oh, I don't mind her hearing what I have to say,' said Alec; 'I would rather she did. The whole world will know soon enough, I fancy,' he added bitterly.

In a few minutes the three were left alone, and Alec told his story.

'So you see the chances are that I shall be accused of a gigantic fraud, and find myself in the dock before long,' he said grimly in conclusion.

'Oh, never!' exclaimed Sophy. 'No one who knows you, no one who had even seen you, would think you capable of such a thing!'

Alec smiled.

'The world is not so good-natured as you are, Miss Meredith.'

Blake did not speak. He was sitting with his elbows on his knees and his head between his hands, studying the pattern of the carpet.

'Had your cousin Semple anything to do with the preparation of the will?' he asked suddenly.

'Nothing whatever,' said Alec. 'He did not even know what its contents were, and insisted upon being in the room to hear it read. I can't help thinking that if I really read out "five hundred thousand pounds," as I thought I did, he would have made a row, instead of going quietly away.'

'But the minister was there too. He would surely have said something if you had read " five thousand,"' remarked Sophy.

'One of them is lying,' said Blake decisively; 'and, of the two, I'm afraid it is more likely to be Semple.'

'Beattie—that is the managing clerk at the office—came up last night and told me all about it,' said Alec. 'He strongly advised me to say nothing to anyone in the meantime—that is, anyone who might appear against me.'

'That was sound advice,' said Blake. 'The only thing that occurs to me to do is to advertise for the man who wrote out the will. He is sure to answer the advertisement. I will see that this is done to-morrow. And I will look you up in the morning, and be ready with another surety, if necessary—you understand.'

'Thank you, Blake. I never thought of that,' said Alec, as he rose to go.

'You must stay here to-night,' said Sophy impulsively; 'you must not think of going out in this fog.'

'Do,' said Blake. 'I'll send a message to your landlady.'

But Alec would not stop. He would be more comfortable at home, he said. They all three went into the hall together.

'Alec, old fellow,' said Blake, putting his hand on the young man's shoulder, 'I'm afraid there's a hard trial in store for you. You will meet it like a man. Don't get excited and lose your head, and don't allow yourself to be too much cast down. Hope for the best. Men have had to face worse things, and have lived through them.'

Alec grasped his friend's hand in silence. Sophy took his left hand between her own.

'You will be brave, and keep up your courage, I know,' she said, as her eyes moistened; 'and we will hope and pray continually that all may yet be well.'

'Oh, all right,' cried Alec, in his old cheery voice. 'As Blake says, men have had such things to bear and worse; why not I? Good-night.'

The touch of sympathy, the evident belief of his friends in his integrity, the cheering words, had made him a new creature.

But there was one house Alec wished to visit before he sought his own solitary abode. After a long drive he found himself at Claremont Gardens. He wished to see Semple, and learn from his own lips whether he had actually read 'five thousand pounds' when he read the will to his uncle. But Semple was, unfortunately, out. Miss Lindsay was in bed with a cold, and Laura received Alec alone.

'I suppose you have heard about this terrible blunder I have committed,' he said, as he took his seat.

'Yes, I was in the dining-room when Mr. Hatchett read the will. Dr. Mackenzie seemed to be in a great passion.'

'I am utterly unable to understand how it occurred,' said Alec; 'I want to see Semple, and ask him a question or two.'

Semple, however, did not come in; and after talking in a desultory way with Laura for some little time, Alec rose to go.

'By the way,' he exclaimed suddenly, '*you* read the will before it was signed; at least, you peeped into it, you remember. Was it not five *hundred* thousand——?'

'Oh, Alec!' exclaimed Laura, clasping her hands upon her breast; 'don't remind me of that! You *said* you would never mention it!'

'I never have mentioned it to a third person, and I never will,' said Alec. 'But I need not ask you how the will read. I have seen it myself.'

'I did not read it—not that part of it, at least,' exclaimed Laura, in some confusion. 'I was only anxious to see what I should have for myself. I had no time to read it. I had hardly time to peep into it. It is cruel, cruel of you to remind me of such a thing!'

'Don't say that, Laura,' said Alec gently. 'Don't cry. Indeed I did not mean to wound you. I only thought that as you had seen the will you might remember—— But it was stupid of me to ask the question, for there is no doubt what the will says. I think I am getting a little bewildered with it all. Last night, when Beattie—that is Mr. Hatchett's managing clerk, you know—told me of what I had done, I felt as if I had been literally bewitched. I could have sworn the will was all right. But never mind. Good-night; and I hope you will forgive me for so thoughtlessly causing you pain.'

So Laura, smiling through her tears, graciously gave him her hand and forgave him; and Alec went away. As soon as the hall-door had closed behind him, she threw herself on the sofa and wept the bitterest tears she had ever known.

Tired out in mind and body, Alec arrived at

his lodgings. On the table lay a piece of blue paper, neatly folded in two. It was a summons for him to appear at the Bow Street Police Court at ten o'clock on the following morning to answer charges of altering a will, and of attempting to obtain money by false pretences.

He hardly heard the voice of the housemaid saying, 'The man told me to give it to you as soon as ever you come in, sir. And please, sir,' the girl added confidentially, for Alec had found favour in her eyes, 'I think he's not gone far away,' and she nodded in the direction of the street.

Alec went to the window, and, shading his eyes with his hand, looked out into the darkness. A burly fellow in plain clothes was loitering at the opposite corner. The house was evidently watched; and the hot blood rushed to the young man's cheek, as he turned away from the window.

'Thank you, Martha. That will do,' he said quietly.

That night Alec felt as though the prison door had already closed behind him.

CHAPTER XXIX.

AT THE POLICE COURT.

THE plan devised by Beattie for securing a fortune for himself and one for his fellow-conspirator, at the expense of the Free Church of Scotland, had been skilfully devised and boldly carried out. Its weakness was due to a succession of unlucky circumstances which could hardly have been foreseen, and which neither Beattie nor James Semple could possibly avert. The clerk's intention had been to draw the will himself, and alter the draft, after it came back from Mr. Lindsay, by taking out the page in which the all-important words appeared, and substituting a fresh page in which the bequest to the

Free Church should be merely five thousand pounds. He would then have examined the draft with the engrossment along with MacGowan, gone to Mr. Lindsay with it, and read aloud 'five hundred thousand pounds,' instead of 'five thousand.' If Mr. Lindsay had insisted on reading the will himself, it would have been easy to pretend that the error was simply due to the carelessness of the clerk who copied it; and if necessary, he could have slipped the original page of the draft back into its place, and thus diverted suspicion from himself. In any case, no one was likely to suspect him, for he had no apparent interest in the matter, one way or the other. If the will were challenged after the old man's death, it would be easy for Semple to say that his uncle had told him to instruct the lawyer's clerk to alter the amount, and easy for Beattie to declare that he had called the testator's attention to the matter when the will was signed.

The fraud seemed very easy of execution, the only real difficulty being the necessity of silencing MacGowan, which did not appear a very arduous undertaking. Beattie was congratulating himself already on his success, when the news that Mr. Lindsay specially desired that his nephew should prepare his will fell on him like a thunderbolt. Should he abandon the scheme? Abandon a hundred thousand pounds! It was not to be thought of. Was there any other method of carrying out the fraud? Beattie could think of none. On the spur of the moment he told Alec Lindsay not to send the draft to be settled by counsel, and not to send it to the law-stationers, hoping that some change in the old man's plans might yet enable him to carry out his scheme.

While Alec was drawing the will, Beattie's subtle brain was devising a way of overcoming this obstacle; and at length he hit upon the plan of getting hold of MacGowan while he was half tipsy, and making him copy the will over again. MacGowan would probably forget next day what he had done in a state of semi-intoxication; but to make sure, he would give him money and send him out of the country.

The strong point of the new scheme was that it involved no risk till the last moment. If it had been found impracticable to substitute the altered will (which Beattie had in his pocket when he went to Claremont Gardens for the second time) for the true one, before the latter was signed, no one could possibly tell that the attempt had been made.

The weak point of the plan was the difficulty of effecting the substitution. After long deliberation, Beattie came to the conclusion that the thing was quite practicable.

Clearly, Alec Lindsay's attention must be diverted by some matter of sufficient importance, at the critical moment; and Beattie partly arranged and partly invented an excuse for seeking him at Mr. Lindsay's house, and making him write an affidavit then and there. Semple, he thought, might insist upon being present while the will was being executed on the score of jealousy of his cousin. He had only to lower the blind, and draw it up again, to make Beattie (who was waiting in a cab at the corner of the street) come upon the scene.

Alec, Beattie argued, was certain at least to come downstairs and see him. He would either leave the will upstairs in his uncle's bedroom, or bring it down with him—probably he would leave it upstairs. Semple was to be in the library when Beattie was shown into it, ready to take the false will from his confederate, and leave the room before Alec entered it. He was then to go upstairs, and try to effect the exchange. If he failed, he failed, and no harm was done. If he found that the will was not there, he was to go back at once to the library, and hand the false will back to Beattie, who was to change one document for the other, while Alec Lindsay was busy with the affidavit.

Everything had been provided for; and everything was carried out according to the conspirators' plans, except that James Semple, instead of fetching the will which Alec had read from his uncle's room, prevailed upon Laura (who had her own reason for wishing to know its contents) to get it and bring it to him. The girl imagined that she was merely helping her lover to ascertain how his uncle had devised his property. Semple, of course, had changed the true will for the false one, as he pretended to read the former at the drawing-room window. When Laura asked him afterwards what he had learned, he replied:

"I couldn't make much of it. I think I shall have a good large sum; but I couldn't be sure that I understood their lawyer's jargon.'

Beattie had not forgotten that on him devolved the responsibility of Alec Lindsay's defence. Thinking it wise to take time by the forelock, he went down to the Temple on the afternoon of the day after the will was read, and made his way to the chambers of Mr. Abel Corker. Mr. Corker's practice lay chiefly in the Bankruptcy Court, but he had seen a good deal of criminal business in his time, and Mr. Beattie was satisfied that he could not intrust young Lindsay's interests to more capable hands than his.

Passing through a very narrow lane, the lawyer's clerk turned into a doorway in an old building, the bricks of which were black with soot. The sides of the doorway were adorned with fifty or sixty names belonging to men learned in the law. Glancing at these to assure himself of being right, Beattie ascended a dark old-fashioned staircase, till he reached the third floor, and stopped at a door embellished with half a dozen names in black letters, and a small knocker.

Mr. Beattie had no sooner rapped than the door was suddenly opened by a small boy who precipitated himself into the aperture, as if determined to block the way until due cause for admittance had been shown.

'Can I see Mr. Corker? I want a consultation,' said the visitor, plunging his hand into his trousers-pocket.

Without speaking a word, the boy led the way into a corner of the passage, boxed off so as to form a clerk's room. This cheerful apartment contained a table and a gas-jet; and the boy watched the stranger in silence as he deposited the regulation sum, one pound six shillings, upon the table. Then, still without uttering a syllable, he went into the passage, and pulled open a door.

Mr. Corker had just come across the street from the Law Courts and had not yet divested himself of his wig and gown. He was standing with his back to the fire, his gown carefully tucked under one arm to save it from being scorched—a needless precaution, as no scorching could make it browner than it was already. His wig, very black, and very much battered, was awry; and his bands looked as if he had forgotten to take them off when he went to bed the night before.

Seeing his visitor, Mr. Corker grunted, left off stroking his chin, and held out two dirty fingers. Mr. Beattie bowed, totally ignoring the fingers, and seated himself without waiting for an invitation to do so.

'I am managing clerk in the firm of Hatchett, Small, and Hatchett,' he began; and went straight on with his story, telling, of course, only what was known to Mr. Hatchett and to Alec himself.

Mr. Corker's keen black eyes were turned full upon the speaker; and as he concluded a benevolent grin overspread the old barrister's sallow features.

'Very neat — very pretty — very pretty *indeed*,' he said. 'This Mr. Lindsay must be a young man of ability. It was not expected, I suppose, that the Scotch minister should be present at the reading of the will?'

'I should think not,' said Mr. Beattie, with a smile.

'And what do they charge him with, eh?'

'They have not had time to charge him yet; but I thought it better to make you acquainted with the facts, so that——'

Mr. Beattie stopped, for Mr. Corker was not listening to him. With one hand still holding up the tails of his gown, and the other caressing the lower part of his face, Mr. Corker was promenading the room, quite oblivious to all but the workings of his own brain.

'And the draft's lost?' he asked suddenly.

'It cannot be found,' said Mr. Beattie gravely.

'That's a mistake. It ought to be found,' said Mr. Corker sharply.

'I'm afraid it cannot be found,' replied Mr. Beattie, and the barrister recommenced his promenade without paying any more attention to his visitor.

Seeing this, Beattie quietly left the room, and after impressing upon the silent clerk the necessity of despatching his master in a hansom to Bow Street Police Court immediately on receiving a telegram, he took his departure.

Next morning Beattie had a note from Alec, posted the night before, telling him of the summons; and in consequence of the managing clerk's forethought, Alec found his counsel awaiting him when he arrived at Bow Street.

The magistrate had not yet taken his seat,

and there was time for a short interview. Etiquette did not require that Mr. Corker should appear in an inferior court such as a police court in professional costume; and this was a pity, for if the barrister had seemed but a faded flower in his wig and gown, he looked positively disreputable without them.

On his part Mr. Corker regarded Alec with considerable interest, very much as an R.A. might look on a young artist who had shown unusual talent.

'There's just one thing I want to say to you, Mr. Corker,' said Alec hurriedly. 'I am convinced now that I made a gross blunder in preparing the will. I could not believe it at first; but I see that I must have done so, and I suppose I must suffer for my carelessness. Whether, in reading the will, I read what was really there, or what I thought was there, I don't know.'

As Alec had been speaking, Mr. Corker kept looking at him with a curious, half-amused, half-admiring expression in his beady black eyes; and when the young man ended his speech he turned slowly away, without answering a word, and began to tell an interesting story to the counsel on the other side. This was Mr. Champneys, a middle-aged man, with a hard, keen face, finely-cut features, and firmly-set thin lips. Mr. Champneys wore well-made clothes and fine linen, and looked like a gentleman. Everything about him was absolutely correct, everything he said was clearly yet cautiously expressed. He sat with unmoved features listening to Mr. Corker's anecdote, when a sudden bustle in the region of the bench announced the arrival of Mr. Mallison, the magistrate. The two barristers and the half-dozen solicitors who were present stood up; and as Mr. Mallison slowly made his way to his chair, Mr. Corker placed his hand over his mouth, and delivered the point of his story into Mr. Champneys' ear, much to that gentleman's disgust.

Alec was sitting beside Beattie at the solicitors' table. He glanced behind him. The court was filled with frowsy women and beetle-browed men, the friends of the prisoners who were presently to appear in the dock, with here and there the tall form of a policeman. A few respectable-looking people were sitting in front; but the majority of those present evidently belonged to the criminal classes; and the unmistakable, sickening odour peculiar to such a crowd filled the air.

'Are these the men with whom I am to live for the future?' said Alec to himself, as a shudder passed over him.

But the magistrate had arranged his papers, and was now ready to begin.

'Are you two gentlemen in the same case?' he asked, with a glance at the two counsel.

'I believe so,' said Mr. Champneys.

'Then we'll take your case first,' answered Mr. Mallison.

This was not pure good-nature on the magistrate's part. He knew Mr. Corker well, and was anxious to get him out of the court as soon as possible.

Then Mr. Champneys rose, and 'opened the case.' Alec's eyes wandered to a kind of box fitted with pews at one side of the bench. Half a dozen men and boys were sitting there, writing as fast as their pencils would go.

'These are the reporters,' thought Alec; 'to-morrow morning my shame will be in every man's mouth.'

As succinctly as he could, Mr. Champneys detailed the facts.

'I shall only ask for a remand to-day,' he

said in conclusion, 'as the documents we rely upon are not yet in our hands. Call the Reverend Dr. Mackenzie.'

Mr. Corker grinned, and looked the magistrate straight in the face.

'I may save the court some trouble,' he said, rising. 'The will is here. The draft seems to have been destroyed as waste-paper. Messrs. Hatchett's managing clerk is here; and he will tell you, sir, that he has searched everywhere for it, and it cannot be found. But to my mind that is of little importance. My client is accused of altering a will. Here is the will. It is evident on the face of it that it has not been altered.'

A long wrangle followed upon this point; and eventually the magistrate decided that he could not commit the defendant upon the charge of altering the will.

'At least, sir,' said Mr. Champneys, 'as the defendant would have gained largely by the fraud, had it not been detected, there was an attempt to obtain money by the false pretence, made in reading the will to his uncle, that the words in the will were " five hundred thousand pounds."'

Another wrangle ensued upon this point, Mr. Corker arguing, with much scorn of his opponent's contentions, that no attempt had yet been made by the accused to get the money, that it could only be obtained from the executors, whereas the alleged false pretence had been made to the testator, and so forth.

After half an hour's argument, Mr. Mallison came to the conclusion that he could not commit the defendant for trial upon that charge, any more than he could upon that of altering the will; and Mr. Corker, muttering his satisfaction, began to fold up the sheet of paper which had done duty as his brief.

Dr. Mackenzie was amazed, bewildered,

shocked. Was the culprit going to escape after all? Was he not to be allowed even to tell his story to the magistrate? He tried to speak to his solicitor; but the solicitor would not listen. He stood up, and laying his hand on his counsel's arm, whispered:

'It was the draft he altered, not the will.'

'Pardon me, sir,' said Mr. Champneys to the magistrate, after a moment's thought; 'it is at least clear that the defendant can be indicted for altering the draft (which would in the circumstances be forgery), and for uttering the forged draft.'

'There's nothing about forgery, or uttering a forged draft here,' said Mr. Corker, with an angry frown, waving the summons in the face of the bench.

'True; but now I apply for a summons. Perhaps your worship would order that it be served at once,' and Mr. Champneys glanced in Alec's direction with a look that was both uneasy and insulting.

Before Mr. Corker could intervene, Alec sprang to his feet.

'I am perfectly willing that the summons should be issued and heard now,' he cried.

Mr. Corker turned upon him with a scowl. Mr. Mallison regarded him gravely over the top of his spectacles.

'You have no objection, I suppose, Mr. Corker,' said the magistrate.

The barrister growled something by way of reply, as he turned to confer with Beattie.

'Seems as if he rather wanted to be locked up,' whispered Mr. Corker.

'I fancy the charge must be heard some time. We gain nothing by delay,' said Beattie, in a low tone.

Mr. Corker gravely unfolded his *pro forma* brief, and placed it before Mr. Beattie, with his finger laid impressively on the title of that document. The other smiled, and, taking up a pen, added the words, 'For Forgery and Uttering a Forged Draft—Mr. Corker—five guineas.' This little point having been satisfactorily settled, the new charge was formally made, and Dr. Mackenzie had the satisfaction of telling his story in the witness-box.

His evidence was evidently that of an honest man, and it told fatally against Alec. Mr. Corker fairly earned his fresh fee, bullying the witness, the counsel for the prosecution, and the magistrate impartially, and loudly contending that as the draft was lost, the evidence was totally insufficient to convict the defendant.

But Mr. Mallison, like many men who have no great strength of mind, was obstinate. He was convinced that a gigantic fraud had been attempted, and he was resolved that the case should go before a jury. Besides, he was getting angry at Mr. Corker's scornful tone and arrogant manner.

'There,' he said, as he signed the warrant of commitment; 'he's fully committed. I suppose you will now conclude your argument, Mr. Corker?'

The barrister dashed the book he was quoting from on the table before him.

'I apply that the defendant may be admitted to bail,' he said. 'I am prepared with bail to any reasonable amount.'

The magistrate shook his head.

'I know Mr. Lindsay well. I will become his bail for twenty thousand pounds,' said a voice from the body of the court.

Alec's pale face flushed with pleasure. It was Blake who had spoken.

But Mr. Mallison had once more made up his mind, and was now immovable.

'Who are you, sir? The defendant has one counsel, and that is enough,' he said to

Blake. 'The case is too important to admit of my considering the question of bail,' he added. 'Half a million sterling, I think you said, Dr. Mackenzie?'

'Half a million, sir.'

'Couldn't think of bail for a moment.'

Mr. Champneys gathered up his books and papers. Mr. Corker, very much disgusted with the turn matters had taken, pushed his way out of court. A policeman touched Alec Lindsay on the shoulder and led him away.

CHAPTER XXX.

ALEC'S FRIENDS VISIT HIM.

It was not until the evening of the following day that a letter from Hubert Blake arrived at the Castle Farm. Alec himself had not written; for Blake had assured him that he would write at once, and would say all that was necessary.

As soon as Alec's father opened the letter and read its opening words, Margaret, who was watching him, saw a change come into his face. She dropped her work and clasped her hands, nerving herself for the bad news which she was sure had come.

The letter was a very long one, and took several minutes to read. Still Margaret waited, without speaking. Suddenly the old man's arm dropped by the side of his chair, and he uttered a sound which was half a moan, half an inarticulate wail.

'What is it, father?' cried Margaret, springing to his side. 'Something dreadful has happened. Oh! what is it?'

Her father gazed at her with stony features, without uttering a word.

'Only tell me, father! Something is wrong with Alec. Is he ill?'

'Worse than that, my girl,' said the old man, almost in a whisper.

'Dead — is he dead? He cannot be dead.'

'It is worse than that,' said Mr. Lindsay, in a louder tone.

'He has——'

The words failed to come.

He conquered his emotion, and spoke them with a cold, cruel distinctness.

'He has stolen—or tried to steal—his uncle's money. He is in prison.'

For a moment Margaret's heart stood still. Then she seized Blake's letter, which was lying on the floor, and began to read it.

The old man sat gazing into the fire without speaking.

'But he may be innocent!' cried Margaret suddenly. 'Mr. Blake does not believe him guilty. See; he says—"Of course I do not for one moment believe——"'

'Of course he says that,' interrupted her father impatiently. 'That is only his polite way of speaking.'

'But he *cannot* be guilty.'

'None of us know what we may do till the temptation comes, Margaret. Besides, it is too clear. Your uncle imagined he was leaving all this money to the Free Church. Alec made him think he was doing so by reading the will wrongly. Dr. Mackenzie has sworn that he heard him do so with his own ears.'

'But James Semple says——'

'I noticed that,' said Mr. Lindsay coldly. 'Don't you see, they would divide this immense sum of money between them? I would not take Semple's word, in such a case, against that of a man like Dr. Mackenzie.'

'Are you going to London, father?' asked the girl, after a pause.

'Ay; I suppose so. In the morning.'

'You will let me go with you?'

'Nonsense, girl. Of what use could *you* be?'

'Not much, perhaps; but we would be company for each other. Oh, father! I can't stay here by myself!'

And the old man yielded a somewhat grudging consent.

Late on the following afternoon they arrived in London. Blake had obtained from his uncle permission to invite them both to Highgate in the first instance, an invitation which Mr. Lindsay was very unwilling to accept. He wished to go to hotel, but Margaret overruled him.

'They will perhaps be offended if we don't go; and we need only stay one night,' she said.

Old Mr. Blake found it convenient to have one of his 'attacks,' as he rather vaguely called them, and thus avoided his guests entirely, Hubert was anxious to make some return for the kindness he had received at Castle Farm; but in spite of his efforts there was a constraint on the little party which nothing could dissipate. Mr. Lindsay looked and spoke very much as usual, except that he was very pale, and there was a stern formality in his manner which forbade any nearer approach. His rough northern accents sounded harsh and forbidding to the southern ears of his new acquaintances.

As for Sophy, her colour heightened a little when she was told that Margaret would accompany her father, and would, for one night at least, be a guest under Mr. Blake's roof. She was anxious to see what the girl was like who had captivated Hubert's affections—for she felt sure that something of the kind had occurred. Margaret's cold pale face, her severe beauty, her low measured tones, took the English girl by surprise.

'She is dressed like a housekeeper,' was Sophy's first thought. 'But how self-possessed she is, how—how unlike anyone I have ever seen,' was her second.

Margaret, in spite of her country-made dress and her utter want of 'style,' was in no way ridiculous. Her calm proud eyes surveyed her hostess, till Sophy felt, somehow, that she was the smaller and weaker creature of the two, and instinctively turned to Hubert for sympathy and protection.

Before Mr. Lindsay went upstairs for the night Blake tried to say a word about Alec, whose name had never crossed his father's lips.

'I think it will be better, Mr. Blake, if we leave that subject entirely alone for the present,' said the old man sternly.

Blake flushed and bit his lip, but made no reply.

'Is it possible that he believes Alec to be guilty?' he said to himself afterwards, with a curious look at his guest's face.

It was true. The laird was not a man to take an imaginative view of things. He looked simply at the facts, and in them he read his son's condemnation. As for the faith that can go beyond 'facts,' the faith that considers a man's character to be the most important of all facts, that can accept a gesture of denial as more potent evidence than the words of many witnesses, he would have looked upon such a thing as childish folly. His son had been tempted, probably by Semple. He had been without true religious principle; and he had fallen. The disgrace was indelible; it was overwhelming. For him no more would the sun shine, or the trees put forth their leaves. His gray hairs would indeed go down with sorrow to the grave.

There was this to be said for him, that he had never known his son. The two natures were in many points absolutely unlike. Their sympathies were diverse. Alec had often abstained from expressing his true opinions, but the old man had nevertheless been quite aware that they were in many instances the antipodes of his own. Confidence between them would in any case have been difficult; and events had made it almost impossible. Alec perhaps did his father less than justice, and the old man felt bitterly that any one of

Alec's chance acquaintances knew his son better than he did himself.

It was a relief to everyone when the travellers retired. Sophy, as she sought her couch, could think of no one but Margaret.

'An iceberg! A positive iceberg!' she exclaimed to herself, as she sat crouching over the tiny fire in her bedroom. 'Even her brother's trouble does not seem to move her in the least. Ah! if I had had such a brother! And Hubert—can he really love her? If it had been anyone worthy of him, anyone who could understand and return his warm affection, I should have been——'

Here Sophy's candle suddenly went out, and her reflections ended in a sigh.

Meanwhile, Alec's naturally buoyant spirits had not failed him. As he told himself over and over again, he had acted like a fool, with a most culpable want of care, and it was only natural and fitting that he should suffer for it.

As for the confinement, the cold of his cell, the mean surroundings, the distasteful food, that mattered little. The disgrace was the worst of it.

'My poor father will feel it terribly,' he said to himself. 'And even if by some accident I am acquitted, will men believe me innocent? How can I hope to rise to a high place in the world's estimation after this? Twenty years hence someone will say — There was some queer story about a will, wasn't there? He was accused of tampering with one, and he was tried at the Old Bailey. I know that.'

This was the thought which chilled him, and nearly broke down his courage. His liberty might be regained; wealth might come in future years; but his good name, more precious than all—was not that irretrievably gone?

This gloomy thought was in his mind one

morning, when his cell-door suddenly opened, and his father appeared, with Margaret behind him.

Alec sprang from his seat, and rushed forward with outstretched hands.

'Father!' he cried.

But the old man had advanced a step or two, and now stood looking at his son immovably, his hands resting on the top of his stick.

'Unhappy boy!'

Alec drew back, his eyes blazing with indignation, unable to speak.

Margaret was seized with a fit of sobbing. It was the only sound in the cell.

'And you believe that I did that?' asked Alec at length, frowning as he spoke.

The lad's look and words almost shook the old man's opinion. Alec seemed to be taking the part of the accuser.

'I believe the oath of God's minister,'

answered Mr. Lindsay. 'Do you—dare you, deny it?'

'Deny it!' echoed the boy, as, turning his back, he looked up at the grated window of his cell.

It was well that his father could not see the look of contempt which was then on his face.

'Speak, sir! Do you deny your guilt to your own father?' cried the old man.

The lad's manner was irritating him past endurance. Alec did not answer at once, and Margaret stepped forward.

'Only say you did not intend to do anything wrong, Alec,' she said, laying her hand on her brother's arm.

'Why should I say it, when I would not be believed, Maggie?' he said in a softer tone. 'We had better not say any more about it. I am sorry you should have had such a long journey in winter for nothing,' he continued, addressing his father. 'Won't you sit down?'

The old man looked at his son without speaking. Was it possible that he could be speaking the truth? No; he told himself. It was not possible. And if so, what a consummate hypocrite, what an impudent scoundrel, had the young man become! And yet he was his son.

The interview lasted a few minutes longer; but nothing further was said on the subject of Alec's guilt or innocence, till the visitors were on the point of leaving the cell.

'Alec,' said the laird in a softer tone than he had yet spoken in, 'if you cannot confess to me, you may at least confess to God. If we confess our sins, you know, He is faithful and just to forgive us our sins. But if any restitution is possible it must be made, else there can be no forgiveness.—Come, Margaret, I think we had better be going now.'

And the old man turned to leave the cell, a hundred-fold more sad at heart than he had been when he entered it.

Alec stood still, in cold but respectful silence. Margaret, as soon as his back was turned, threw one arm round her brother's neck; but he did not respond to her embrace.

'And you, Maggie? Do you believe this of me?'

'Not—not if you say you did not intend to do wrong, Alec. But if you had done it, I would have loved you all the same,' she said in a hurried whisper.

'Thank you, Maggie. But—never mind. Good-bye for to-day. Don't let father come again, if you can help it.'

In another moment they were gone.

So even Maggie did not quite believe in him. She was not sure. She was balancing probabilities.

'And who will believe in my innocence, if my own father does not?' he cried aloud, when he found himself alone.

Who indeed? Alec saw, as he had not seen before, the cruel strength of the very accusation to blast his life. Henceforth an honourable distinction was impossible for him. In a moment the ambition which, vague as its shape had been, had been the life-blood of his soul, perished within him. He saw the years stretch out before him, without hope of any second spring. His love was wrecked; his good name was gone; and, worst of all, there was nothing to live for.

All at once he burst into a wild fit of laughter.

The gaoler came and opened his cell-door to see what was the matter.

'It's a queer world this, isn't it, turnkey?'

'None the less queer for having *you* in it,' said the man, as he shut the door with a bang, and made the heavy bolts fall into their sockets.

CHAPTER XXXI.

MISGIVINGS.

MEANTIME, James Semple's conscience had been making him very miserable. It was not the fraud that troubled him. He had long since made up his mind that to prevent his uncle's unnatural intentions from being carried out was a very venial offence. Nor was it merely Alec's incarceration. That, he thought, would be amply compensated by the quarter of a million which would fall to his share as one of the residuary legatees. Alec's fortune, in fact, would be twice as large as his own; and it was only fair that he should take his share of the inconveniences which were inseparable from the securing of it.

But if his cousin should be convicted, and sentenced to a long term of penal servitude, Semple knew that he would feel very uncomfortable indeed. Yet, he argued, Alec would certainly have himself to thank if that was the result. If he had chosen to take Beattie's hint, and declare that his uncle, before he died, had privately told him that he had changed his mind, and wished to leave the bulk of his money to his two nephews, all would have been well, and Dr. Mackenzie might have raged as much as he pleased, without being able to do any harm. It was Alec's inability to explain the discrepancy between the will as it stood and his uncle's known intentions which formed the real strength of the prosecution.

It would be very sad if Alec were convicted in consequence of his own obstinacy, but it would be still more sad, it would be a quite intolerable calamity, if anything should happen to Mr. James Semple. And in spite of Beattie's assurances, he felt far from secure. He was horrified to find that Alec was actually in prison before he had heard that criminal proceedings had been thought of. If the fraud were discovered, what would be his fate?

'I say, Beattie,' he said to his friend one day, 'I almost think I'll take a voyage to California, or somewhere, and stay there till this affair has been thoroughly forgotten. You could remit my share of the proceeds, couldn't you?'

Beattie looked at him curiously.

'I might. But I should be much more likely to remit a detective officer.'

'What!' cried the other with a white, scared face. 'You don't mean that you would turn traitor, do you?'

'I mean that you would turn traitor if you bolted just now. Don't you see that it would make everybody believe that you had done something, and that you were afraid you would be found out? Besides, we need your evidence for your cousin's trial.'

Semple muttered something to the effect that Alec's trial could get on very well without him.

'But you don't think they can convict him?' he said aloud.

'Corker says he thinks he can get him off, and he's the best criminal lawyer in the country,' answered Beattie tranquilly. 'But you mustn't talk of a trip to America,' he added, with a meaning look. 'If you do, you will never see one penny of your uncle's money. I'll see to that.'

'Oh; I was only joking, of course,' said the other, as he took his leave.

Semple was still living at Claremont Gardens, and he made his way thither that day, after parting from his companion.

As he opened the door with his latch-key, Laura met him in the hall.

'Oh, James,' she whispered to him, 'Margaret Lindsay has come up to town; and she is in the drawing-room now, with your aunt. She is waiting on purpose to see you.'

Semple muttered an oath between his teeth, as he very deliberately took off his overcoat; and Laura glided back to the drawing-room.

'No, my dear,' Miss Lindsay was saying when she entered; 'nothing will ever make me believe such a thing o' Alec. If your feyther has his doots, as ye seem to think, he has less gumption than I gied him credit for. Hoots! The thing's perfeckly ridiculous!' exclaimed the old lady, smoothing away imaginary crumbs from her lap as she spoke.

Margaret felt more cheered by this speech

than she had been since the blow had fallen; and at that moment Semple entered the room.

'How do you do, Maggie?' he said, going up to her in a hurried way, and shaking her by the hand. 'I didn't know you had come up. Almost a pity, I think; for this scrape, I mean this ridiculous accusation they have made against your brother, is a matter of no real moment. It is only a temporary—inconvenience, you know.'

The three women were listening to him in silence, and somehow his words sounded hollow and unreal, even to himself.

Margaret felt hurt that her wound should thus be openly probed and commented on, and she made no reply.

'Then you think that Mr. Alec Lindsay is in no real—danger?' asked Laura timidly.

Semple turned to her almost gratefully.

'Not the least in the world,' he said

eagerly. 'I have just seen B—— Mr.—a —the lawyer, you know, and he feels quite sure about it.'

'Oh, I am so glad!' exclaimed Laura.

Then there was a pause.

'There is just one question I should like to ask you, James,' said Margaret.

Semple's heart sank within him.

'When Alec read over the will, did he read the bequest "five thousand" or "five *hundred* thousand" pounds?'

'Five thousand,' said Semple promptly.

'Are you sure?' asked Margaret, her large eyes steadily regarding him.

'I'll take my oath of it.'

'But Alec says, I understand, that he either said, or meant to say, "five *hundred* thousand."'

'There's no doubt he read it as it stands —five thousand—and I heard him,' persisted Semple. 'But there seems to have been a mistake of some sort. I don't profess to understand it myself.'

'Umph,' said Miss Lindsay.

'Let us hope for the best, dear Margaret —I may call you Margaret, as I did in the old days, mayn't I?' said Laura, when Margaret rose to go. 'And you will let me help you to look for rooms, won't you?'

But Margaret was in no mood to accept civilities. She thanked Laura rather coolly, and went away, declining her cousin's offer to escort her to Highgate.

'Have you been to see Alec, James?' asked Miss Lindsay, when Margaret had gone.

Now this was what Semple had not been able to bring himself to do.

'Not yet,' he said sullenly. 'He doesn't want a lot of people bothering round him. At least, if I were in his place I wouldn't.'

'If you were in his place——' repeated the old lady, as if she were not thinking of her words, as she turned and slowly left the room.

Semple shuddered, and watched her curiously till the door closed behind her.

'James,' said Laura suddenly, 'you remember one night, before my uncle died, you asked me to watch what he did with a paper that had come from the lawyers. What was in that paper? Had it anything to do with the will?'

'What paper? Oh, I remember now. No; nothing in the world.'

Laura had purposely put her question in this shape.

'James, you are not telling me the truth,' she said, looking at him steadily. 'You gave me to understand at the time that it had to do with it.'

'You are quite mistaken,' cried Semple, greatly alarmed.

It was the manner of his denial which the

clever girl had wished to observe; and what she saw satisfied her that she had been right in her guess about the paper.

'My uncle put it in his desk,' she said slowly, 'and I told you how to take the desk out of the room. Did you get the paper? What did you do with it? Did you burn it?'

'No—no! What makes you imagine such things?'

'I believe you did burn it. Come now!' she said, laughing.

Semple laughed a little too, and looked furtively at his companion, as she sat looking into the fire. Laura turned round sharply, and caught his glance, smiled to herself, and gracefully changed the subject.

Seeing that the danger had gone by, Semple ventured to take her hand. Laura quietly withdrew it.

'What's the matter, Laura?'

'Nothing.'

'Why do you treat me like that?'

'How else should I treat you?'

'Aren't we two engaged?'

'Not that I know of.'

'But we are,' cried Semple, catching her wrist.

'Indeed you are mistaken,' said the girl, throwing off his grasp. 'You asked me, I know.'

'And you accepted me.'

'I have not made up my mind about it yet.'

'Upon my word!'

His astonishment prevented his saying more. Suddenly a thought occurred to him, which stung him like a serpent.

'Oh, I suppose that means that you have heard.'

'Heard what?'

'That Alec Lindsay is a residuary legatee

as well as I.' In a moment he saw that he had made a great mistake. She had not known it before. But he was too angry to think of what he said. 'If the poor fellow escapes penal servitude, that is,' said he, with a sneer.

Laura Meredith rose and drew a step nearer to the smiling, mocking face before her. She could gladly have struck it. Then she moved away again, while the smile died from Semple's face; and without uttering another word, she walked out of the room.

Semple, in a rage, went off to his club, banging the door behind him; and Laura, as soon as she saw that the coast was clear, slipped back to the drawing-room fire (for, cat-like, she dearly loved a good blaze), and sat down to think.

'So Alec, if he was not found guilty, was to be rich after all—as rich as his cousin! What a good thing it was that she had not committed herself definitely to Semple! But Alec —would he ever come back to her? She remembered only too well the look in his face when he met her outside Mr. Lindsay's bedroom door with the will in her hand.

Yet, if he were the victim of a plot, and if she were to deliver him from the snare in which he had been taken, surely gratitude would make him turn to her then! And she would be a good wife to him; faithful, and true, and loving. How happy they might be! And the girl's eyes softened as the idea crossed her mind.

He must be set free, and she must do it. He was innocent. She had never doubted that. (Curiously enough, this girl had judged Alec better than his own father had done.) How had he been involved? Had he really made a mistake? Or was there some conspiracy on foot?

Laura went the right way to work. She

did not stop to consider the difficulties of the case, but went straight to motives. If there was a plot on foot, Semple was concerned in it. She felt sure of that.

Why had he been so anxious to get hold of that paper? She believed he had burned it.

Then, why had he wanted to see the will, when (as she afterwards learned) he had been in the room while it was read? Had he made any alteration in it? No. She felt certain there had been no time for anything of that kind. If he had even bent down to write in it, she must have seen him doing it. He had only stood at the window with it in his hand reading it. Besides, if he had altered the writing in any way, the alteration must have been noticed.

The girl's subtle mind was at fault. She could see no clue to the plot which, she felt certain, existed.

Suddenly she remembered the conversation between Semple and a stranger, which she had partly overheard at the railway-station. 'We are not out of the wood yet,' the stranger had said; and 'he must not be there when the will is read, on any account.' Who must not be there? Not Alec, surely. Dr. Mackenzie? Why? Clearly, that he might not be able to say what Alec had read.

So much seemed clear; but still there was no explanation of the fact that Alec had failed to carry out his uncle's instructions. Ponder over it as she might, the girl could not solve the mystery.

'But suppose I were to write to Alec and tell him all this,' she said to herself, 'or tell some friend of his, Mr. Blake, for example, and get him to tell the lawyer; he might be able to put the pieces of the puzzle together. If they have made up some plot and allowed the blame to fall on Alec, what a shame!' And again a pleased look came into her face as she remembered how Alec's gratitude, if she were the means of establishing his innocence, would surely bring him once more to her side.

But—how could she have overlooked it? She could never tell this. She had made herself one of the conspirators. How could she confess that she had kept a watch on the old man, and told his nephew where his private papers were to be found? Could she tell openly that she had smuggled his will out of his room before it was signed, and had given it to Semple to read? She might find herself in the dock instead of Alec, accused of—she knew not what. Who would believe that she had done these things innocently, when she could give no good reason for doing them at all?

Was she going to risk standing her trial with Semple, and——? She shuddered, shook her head, and crept upstairs to her own room. She dared not tell.

CHAPTER XXXII.

BEFORE THE TRIAL.

'Well, old fellow, how are you getting on?'

Alec turned on the rough bed which served him for a couch in the daytime, and saw Hubert Blake.

'Not getting on at a particularly fast pace just at present,' said Alec, as he got up and shook hands with his friend.

'You're keeping up your spirits, I hope?'

'I do my best.'

'How do you amuse yourself?'

'I got the doctor to lend me an old Todhunter. I find nothing like algebra for making the time pass—that is, if you try to find out something of it for yourself.'

'What have you got here?' asked Blake, who had strolled up to a corner where a card was hanging.

'Only an almanac.'

'And you're ticking off the days, I see. Are you counting up to the—— ?'

'The day of my trial—yes,' said Alec, looking as if he wished that his friend had not been so observant.

'Are you so anxious for it to come off?' asked Blake, sitting down on the edge of the bed.

'Yes. Naturally I want to know the worst.'

'I was talking with your lawyer friend yesterday. He seems certain that you will be acquitted.'

'An acquittal would not set things right.'

'What?'

'Don't you see that whether I am convicted or not is a thing that affects only my liberty and my personal comfort? If I am acquitted it will probably be by some of those legal arguments which Mr. Corker used before the magistrate. They may be sound or unsound; it doesn't matter one straw. How far does an acquittal of that kind go to clear one's character?'

Blake murmured something vague and deprecatory.

'Or it may be that the jury may "give me the benefit of the doubt." Will *that* set me right with the world? No, Blake. My life is ended, almost before it has begun.'

'Don't say that, Lindsay. At the worst you can emigrate, and——'

'And hide myself. Yes, to be sure. I could do that.'

'I'll tell you what I wish you would do for me,' said Alec, after a pause. 'Get my father to go back to Scotland. He cannot possibly do me any good. He——' Alec stopped and bit his lip. He was ashamed to say that his father believed him guilty.

'It is natural for him to wish to be here,' began Blake.

'He comes here and preaches at me,' said Alec. 'I dare say he means very well; but I really *cannot* stand it. I think it is taking a mean advantage of circumstances, for I can't run away, and I can't very well tell him to leave me alone.'

'Can't you listen in patience?'

'You see, I've got the chaplain on to me too.'

'I used to think you were rather fond of religious discussions,' said Blake maliciously.

Alec laughed. It was a hard joyless sound, not pleasant to hear.

'The worst of it is, my two spiritual guides give contrary directions,' he said. 'But you have absolutely no conception how unpleasant it is to sit here and be preached at. Of the two I think I like the chaplain best. Professional training always tells, and——'

'Alec,' interrupted Blake, who wanted to change the subject, '*can* you imagine how that word "hundred" slipped out of that will?'

'It never was there,' said Alec.

Blake shook his head.

'Or it would be there now.'

'You see the whole thing was left to me,' Alec went on. 'No one so much as touched it, except myself and——'

Suddenly he remembered something—the little incident of Laura's curiosity. He paused rather awkwardly, considering whether it could possibly affect the matter, and decided that it was absolutely of no importance. He opened his lips to mention the circumstance as an excuse for his sudden silence, when he remembered that it was not very creditable to Laura, and besides, that he had promised her he would never speak of what she had done. He stopped again, when on the point of speaking, and looking up, he caught a surprised and troubled expression in his friend's face. Meeting Alec's gaze, Blake dropped his eyes. He saw that something was being concealed from him, and he had imagined that he had known every incident connected with the making of the will.

'Blake is beginning to doubt me,' said Alec to himself. 'Soon I shall have no one left.' When he next spoke, his voice, in spite of himself, was hard and repelling. He was too proud to give an explanation of his reticence; and Blake, on his side, was afraid to ask for any. When he left the prison he had not come to believe in his friend's guilt; but his faith was shaken.

'I won't say I distrust him; and yet—it is very queer.' That was the tenor of his thoughts. He felt profoundly sorry for Mr.

Lindsay, and tried to persuade him to return to Scotland before the trial. But this would not have suited the old man's ideas of his duty as a father. He would stay by his son, guilty though he were, to the end.

Alec, of course, had his despairing moods, moods in which there seemed no brightness for him, nor any possibility of comfort, in heaven or on earth; and as the imprisonment began to tell more and more upon his health these periods became more frequent and more prolonged. It was not surprising, indeed, that sometimes a deep melancholy seized him, as it were in a grasp of iron.

He was sitting in his cell one day, holding a book before him, but reading nothing, while his mind was lost in aimless, gloomy wanderings, when he heard the familiar sound of the unlocking of his door.

'Oh, can't they leave me alone even one day!' he groaned to himself.

A tall figure in an immense cloak entered.

'Cameron!'

The two men stood grasping each other's hands in silence. Alec's mobile lips were working strangely. As for Cameron, a great beard effectually concealed the expression of his mouth, but his eyes were moist.

Then he broke into a laugh. and withdrawing his hand gave Alec a shove which sent him staggering backwards.

'What on earth made ye get into such a pickle?'

· That's just what I want to know.'

'Come now, tell me all about it,' said Cameron, seating himself on the bed.

'If you don't mind, old fellow, I'd rather not,' said Alec. 'You see, I've had to go over these wretched details so often ; and I can hardly help thinking of them night and day, so it is a relief to speak of something else. Tell me about yourself. What are you doing now?'

'I'm assistant to Dr. Farquharson. But I don't care for the work. I can scarcely prevent myself from pitching some of the patients out of the windows of their own bedrooms. They have nothing in the world the matter with them but over-feeding and too much coddling. Occasionally I give them the nastiest drugs I can think of, by way of relieving my feelings, especially castor oil.'

'You brute!'

'I am only fit for surgery. I hate the pill-and-powder business.'

'How did you come to be in London?' asked Alec suddenly.

'I wanted to see what the London hospitals are like.'

'Duncan, ye're leein',' said Alec gravely.

'Maybe I am; an' maybe I'm no. That's neither here nor there.'

'You saw something about—about it in the papers, didn't you?'

'Lees an' trash.'

'Well, I'm not so sure about that;' and Alec, having thus reached the subject, told the whole story of the will. 'And now, doesn't it look very like as if I had struck that word " hundred " out of the draft?'

For answer Cameron gave a comical look, and slowly shook his head.

'Ye haven't brains enough, laddie, to be a thief.'

Alec looked anxiously at his friend, with searching eyes. Cameron bore the look unmoved. Yet Alec was not satisfied.

'Do you think it *possible* that I made a blunder like that unintentionally?' A wild thought came into the lad's head, and he uttered what was in his mind. 'What if I were to tell you that I did it on purpose?' he asked.

It seemed almost as if he were bent on

destroying the faith of the only man who still believed in him.

'Do you mean wilfully, after time for reflection, taking a day or two over it?'

Alec nodded.

'I should certify that you were insane.'

'God bless you, Cameron!'

'Man, you're half cracked already, to talk in that way. Your uncle was a donnart auld eediot. That's undeniable. And if ye confessed to me that being suddenly aware of the injustice he meant to do you (as I look on it), you had thrown his will on the fire, I might have thought that possible enough. But if you were to tell me that you sat down in cold blood, and thought out this plan for yourself, and determined to carry it out, and did carry it out, I would *not* believe you. I should say ye were mad first.'

'Cameron, my father——' began Alec after a pause.

'No?'

The word was accompanied by a raising of the eyebrows, and followed by slow shakes of the head, which indicated that in his opinion some people were hopelessly stupid.

'He'll be very sorry, and ashamed of his want of trust in you, Alec; don't forget that,' said Cameron.

'My innocence may never be known. My character is gone already,' said the prisoner, glad to tell what was in his heart to a sympathetic ear.

'That's not certain,' said Cameron quickly, as he grasped his friend by the shoulder, and scanned his face narrowly. 'And if it were, why, better men than you have had to thole* the same thing.'

'That's true. I shouldn't make so much of it. But, you see, I have so little here to occupy my thoughts.'

* To bear.

'I'll come and see you again, if they'll let me. But I don't think they will. It was a fashious* job to get in. But I'll be in court. You may depend on that.'

'No, no, Duncan. You must go back to your work.'

'I haven't left the sick folk as sheep without a shepherd, which they would be if they were left entirely to old Farquharson. So I chose a sub-deputy-assistant before I came away. A fourth-year's student just scraped through. An Englishman, and I think the most ignorant man I ever came across, but popular with the women. Yes, yes, man, in a minute,' he said impatiently to the turnkey, who opened the door to say that the allotted time had expired. 'That minds me I would practise my art on you, Alec, my lad, if time permitted. *Fiat experimentum*, ye ken.'

* Troublesome.

'There's nothing the matter with me,' said Alec.

'I don't like that cough. And you're very thin. I must see the pill-man of this institution mysel'. I suppose they keep an animal of that kind on the premises?'

'I don't know, I'm sure. I suppose so. Good-bye, old fellow. You've done me a world of good.'

'After all this rumpus and palaverin's by,' said Duncan, 'I'll carry ye off *vi et armis* to the island of Scalpa, and fatten you up there for a month; or, better still, send you for a voyage to Australia—Coming! I tell ye, ye——'

The rest of the speech was lost in the dark recesses of the Gaelic language, as Dr. Cameron strode after the bulky form of the turnkey.

One good result of this visit was that Alec was removed next day to the hospital ward of the prison.

CHAPTER XXXIII.

THE TRIAL.

A THICK, murky fog hung over London on the morning of Alec Lindsay's trial. Waves of chill mist rolled up from the river, and met the sulphurous vapours which filled the air. The sun was not visible at all. In every street and building gas was flaming, as if it had been midnight. Rain or snow would have been a relief from the stifling yellow vapour; but neither fell. The cold, clammy, omnipresent fog reigned supreme.

As it happened, Hubert Blake had slept at his uncle's the night before. He had, of course, determined to be present at the trial; and when he came down to breakfast, an hour earlier than usual, he was surprised to see that both Sophy Meredith and Miss Elmwood were dressed ready to go out.

'You are not thinking of shopping on a day like this?' asked Hubert in some surprise.

'No, indeed,' answered Sophy, almost indignantly. 'We are going to the court.'

Blake said no more at the time; but when Miss Elmwood had left the breakfast-room to put on her bonnet, he returned to the subject.

'I really think you had better stay at home,' he said, in a matter-of-fact way. 'It is quite unnecessary for you to be there, and it may be a very painful scene.'

Sophy's fingers were trembling nervously, as she played with the sugar-tongs. She was obliged to fold her hands, and pause for a second or two before she answered:

'I think, if there is ever a time when one

should stand by one's friends, it is when they are———'

And then she stopped, as if she could not trust herself to say more.

'Yes, of course; but, you see, you can't do Lindsay any good by going; probably he won't even know you are there. It is not as if you were a relation of his.'

It was all true enough; and Sophy felt only too keenly that her action would seem ridiculous; yet she was none the less determined to go. She had nothing to say in reply, and sat searching her mind for some excuse, while the tears that would no longer be restrained rapidly filled her eyes.

Blake saw her agitation with surprise.

'I had no idea she was so tender-hearted,' was his first thought. 'Can it be that—that Lindsay is something more than a friend to her?' was his second. 'She is older than he is, but not so very much older, after all. It would not be so very surprising, if it were so. It would be——'

Then his thoughts became more vague. He could not imagine what his uncle's house would be like without Sophy as its mistress. There would be no one to chat to about his pictures, no one to whom he could bring the gossip of the little world of artists to which he had returned. As for the wandering, unsettled life he had been living the year before, he thought of it now with positive disgust. Yes; if Sophy were to go out of his life, she would leave a sad blank behind.

He did not stop to consider on what a slender foundation he was thus constructing the future. Sophy was surprised at his silence, and glanced at him timidly. He seemed lost in reflection; then suddenly looking up, their eyes met. He was astonished that she looked so beautiful. He had never thought of her as pretty before; but indeed the tender light in her eyes, and the faint colour coming suddenly into her pale cheeks would have made a far plainer face seem fair.

'Don't you think we had better be going?' said Hubert, in a gentle tone. 'The court may be crowded; and we may find a difficulty in getting seats.'

Sophy rose and left the room without saying anything more.

The fog detained the party from Highgate, so that when they reached the court it was with difficulty that Blake could find seats for his friends. To Sophy the scene was so new and strange, and the effect of the fog so bewildering, that in spite of the gas jets flaring here and there it was some time before she could make out anything distinctly. By degrees she distinguished the Judge in his ermine-trimmed gown, the City dignitaries in their robes of office, the officials of the court on their raised seats under the bench, and the empty jury-box. But the object which fascinated her was the high, spiked iron railing which surrounded a wide space in the centre of the court, facing the bench. That, she knew, was the dock.

It was tenanted by one person, a woman, a forlorn-looking creature, with a dirty shawl thrown over her bare head. On either side of her, but a little behind, stood a policeman. For some minutes after Sophy and her companions took their seats, there was perfect silence in the building, so that they wondered what the reason could be. Then the voice of the Judge broke the stillness.

'The sentence of the court is that you be kept in penal servitude for the period of seven years.'

Sophy did not know what the woman's offence had been, but the punishment seemed terrible; and as the poor creature, who had evidently not expected so long a term, broke out into cries, oaths, and imprecations, Sophy shuddered, and was almost moved to tears. To the Judge, to the barristers, the police, and the other officials, it was only part of the ordinary routine of their lives. To the gentle woman who had lived in shelter all her days, the sight of this sister-woman's face, coarse, bloated, distorted by passion and despair, was like a glimpse into a world of which she had never even dreamed—a world in which blessings were exchanged for curses, tender thoughts for the fury of selfish passions, and liberty for bondage.

As the woman was led down a staircase inside the dock, which communicated with the cells, the clerk of the arraigns and the counsel on the front row were exchanging a few words. And in another moment the clerk called out:

'Bring up Alexander Lindsay!'

A subdued rustle of excitement passed through the court, and every eye was turned to the dock. In another moment Alec had taken his place, calm and self-possessed, but very pale. The first thing he saw was his father's face. The old man was sitting at the solicitor's table, facing the dock, with Margaret by his side. No emotion of any kind was visible on his features; but Alec fancied—probably it was only his fancy—that a look of reproach was in his eyes. Margaret, unable to meet her brother's gaze, was looking stedfastly at the table in front of her. Opposite her sat Beattie; and behind him, with his back to Alec, sat Mr. Corker, who had, of course, been instructed for the defence.

As the clerk was reading the indictment, Alec's eyes were fixed on the ledge in front of him. He knew that Duncan Cameron was somewhere in the building; and the thought comforted him. Then, somehow, he fell to thinking of his College-days ; and was only recalled from his reverie when the clerk's voice was raised to ask him :

'How say you, Alexander Lindsay ; are you guilty, or not guilty ?'

'Not guilty.'

Then the clerk proceeded to swear in the jury ; and then Mr. Collithorne, Q.C., rose to open the case for the Crown.

Mr. Collithorne was famed at the bar for his 'deadly moderation' as a prosecuting counsel. Never raising his voice, over-stating nothing, admitting beforehand the facts on which he knew the defence would be based, his words had with the jury the weight which attaches to the utterances of a Judge rather than that which belongs to the speech of an advocate.

'May it please your worship,' he began. 'Gentlemen of the jury, this is a very painful case, and one which well deserves that close and careful attention which I am sure you will bestow upon it. Fortunately the facts are few and simple. The prisoner is a grand-nephew of the late Mr. James Lindsay, who, as some of you may know, was a very wealthy man. Some time before his death, Mr. Lindsay conceived the idea of bequeathing by his will a large sum of money, no less than half a million sterling, to the religious body of which he was a member, the Free Church of Scotland. He talked over that intention with an old friend of his, the Reverend Dr. Mackenzie, of Glasgow; and (though that is not really important to the matter in hand) Dr. Mackenzie will tell you that he neither suggested this idea to Mr. Lindsay nor in any way pressed him to make this bequest.

'Having settled in his mind the disposition which he intended to make of his property,

Mr. Lindsay sent to his solicitors, asking them to call and take instructions for his will. His solicitors were Messrs. Hatchett, Small, and Hatchett, a most respectable firm; and I must tell you that the prisoner was at that time a clerk in Messrs. Hatchett's office. Well, the solicitors sent their managing clerk, a Mr. Beattie, to take Mr. Lindsay's instructions. We have subpœnaed this Mr. Beattie; and I have no doubt he will tell you that Mr. Lindsay distinctly informed him that the bequest to the Free Church of Scotland was to be five hundred thousand pounds. The paper on which these instructions were written by Mr. Beattie was sent to Mr. Lindsay with the draft-will, and was not returned by him. It was not found among the testator's papers. Probably Mr. Lindsay, thinking that it was of no importance, destroyed it.'

Mr. Collithorne then went on to speak of

Mr. Lindsay's request that his nephew should personally prepare his will, and of the fact that the prisoner actually did write the draft with his own hand. 'That fact, gentlemen,' he continued, 'will hardly be disputed; and if it is not admitted I will prove it to you by unimpeachable evidence. The draft itself, as well as the man who engrossed it, has disappeared. It ought to have been found with other drafts of a like nature in the prisoner's room. It has been searched for, and cannot be found. But while it was in Mr. Lindsay's possession, before he returned it to the solicitors to be engrossed, it was seen and read by Dr. Mackenzie, whom I shall place in the box before you. He will tell you, gentlemen, that it was in the prisoner's handwriting, and that it contained a bequest of five hundred thousand pounds to certain trustees for the Free Church of Scotland. He will tell you that he read it most carefully, and that the sum was written both in figures and in words. The draft was sent back on the very night it arrived, Dr. Mackenzie posting it with his own hand.

'Now, gentlemen, it is a singular fact, that, so far as we have been able to learn, not a single individual in Messrs. Hatchett's office saw that draft, except the prisoner and a clerk named MacGowan, who engrossed the will; and the theory of the prosecution is, that before handing the draft to MacGowan to engross the prisoner struck out of it the all-important word "hundred," so that the bequest should run "five thousand pounds" only. Inquiries for this clerk, MacGowan, have been made in all directions; but from the day he engrossed that will he never turned up at the office; he disappeared from his lodgings on the following day, and has not since been heard of.

'We come now to the actual execution of

the will. It was brought to Mr. Lindsay's house by the prisoner. It was read over to the testator by the prisoner; and, in reading it, the prisoner inserted the word "hundred," which was not in the will, before the word "thousand," thus leading his uncle, the testator, to imagine that the will was really in accordance with his intentions. This fact will be proved to you on the evidence of Dr. Mackenzie; and it will be for you to judge whether he could possibly be mistaken on a point of such importance, a point on which his attention would naturally be fixed.

'It is only right that I should tell you, gentlemen,' continued the barrister, 'that there was one other person in the room when the will was read besides the testator, the prisoner, and the witness I have named. And you may be surprised to hear that this person does not bear out the statement which the Reverend Mr. Mackenzie will make on oath before you, as to what the prisoner did actually read from the will.'

Here Mr. Corker interposed, and said something in an angry tone to Mr. Collithorne.

'Perhaps my friend is right, gentlemen,' said the Queen's Counsel, majestically waving the Old Bailey barrister back into his seat. 'It may be better for him to deal with his own witness, if he should think it worth while to call him. You will understand, gentlemen, later on, the reason of my learned friend's interposition.

'As I said at the commencement of my observations, this is a painful case. I do not remember that, in all my experience, I have had to do with a prosecution in which one's natural sympathies would be more strongly excited in favour of the prisoner. His youth and his character, hitherto blameless, will naturally and properly tell in his favour. It would only be natural, also, if you found yourselves sympathizing with the keen feelings of disappointment with which a young man would hear of an intention on the part of an uncle to alienate the greater part of his fortune from those who may reasonably have looked forward to inheriting it. But these sympathies you are, for the present, bound to forget. Your one thought must be—Did the accused commit the offence with which he is charged? As to the motive for the crime, you must remember that the prisoner is one of the residuary legatees under the will; in other words, the alteration in the legacy would put the sum of two hundred and forty-seven thousand five hundred pounds into the prisoner's pocket. Crimes much more serious than this have been committed ere now for the tenth part of such a sum, by men who had, up to the moment of temptation, led innocent lives. If you can, after hearing the evidence, entertain a reasonable, a serious doubt of the prisoner's guilt, you will, of course, let him have the benefit of it. But if the facts as proved point irresistibly, in your opinion, to the conclusion that the offence of which he is accused was committed by him, it will be your duty—however painful that duty may be—to say so by your verdict.'

A faint rustle passed over the court as Mr. Collithorne sat down. Cameron, who from his corner could see the faces of the jurymen, noticed that they wore a very serious look. And Alec ? He knew that the counsel for the Crown had spoken nothing but the truth ; and his heart died within him. He felt that his character was ruined irretrievably in the eyes of the world. He could almost have wished that the formalities of the trial could be omitted and sentence pronounced at once, that he might hide himself from the cold and curious eyes around him in the quiet seclusion of his cell.

The first witnesses called were the servants who had witnessed the will. The junior counsel for the Crown, a young gentleman with a very new wig and a very nervous manner, asked them the necessary questions, and Mr. Corker did not think it worth while to cross-examine them.

'Call Mr. William Beattie,' said Mr. Collithorne, and that gentleman rose from his seat at the solicitors' table, and slowly made his way to the witness-box. As he did so, Mr. Corker broke into a lively argument — nominally addressed to the Judge, but really aimed at the jury—on the lawfulness of the Crown calling the managing clerk of the defendant's solicitor as a witness. The Judge, however, ruled—as Mr. Corker quite expected that he would rule—that Mr. Beattie might be questioned as to matters which came to his knowledge before the relationship of attorney and client began, and Mr. Beattie was sworn.

Speaking in a low but clear tone, Mr. Beattie said, in answer to Mr. Collithorne's questions, that he had received instructions from the late Mr. Lindsay as to his will; that these instructions included a legacy of five hundred thousand pounds to the Free Church of Scotland; that, in accordance with Mr. Hatchett's directions, he handed the paper on which these instructions were jotted down to the defendant; and, finally, that the missing draft had been searched for in the prisoner's room and in the office generally, and had not been found.

'One word more, Mr. Beattie,' said Mr. Collithorne; 'at that time was there a clerk in Messrs. Hatchett's office named MacGowan?'

'There was.'

'Look at the will. In whose handwriting is it?'

'In his handwriting—MacGowan's.'

'Did he return to the office after he engrossed that will?'

'He did not. When he did not come back that afternoon, a letter was written dismissing him.'

'What was his character?'

'I know nothing against his character, except that he was unsteady. He would have been dismissed before, but——'

'Yes. But what?'

'But Mr. Lindsay interceded for him, and the offence was overlooked.'

'You mean the prisoner?'

'Yes.'

A subdued murmur ran round the court as these words were spoken. Then there was a silence.

'That was months before,' added Mr. Beattie; but the impression had already been created that there had been a friendship or, at least, a relationship of patronage on the one side, and gratitude on the other, between the man who was now alleged to have altered the draft, and the man who, after engrossing the will from it, had suddenly disappeared.

Then Mr. Collithorne sat down, and Mr. Corker got up.

'Did Mr. Lindsay express any hesitation when he said that he wished to leave so large a sum to the Free Church?'

'Not in words.'

'In any other way?'

'By his manner he did. He spoke in a hesitating way, as if he had hardly made up his mind.'

'Judging from his manner, did you expect that he would perhaps alter these instructions?' asked the Judge.

'I quite expected it, my lord.'

Mr. Corker looked hard at the jury, to see that they paid due attention to this answer, and then proceeded:

'Now, as to the search for the draft. The drafts made in your office are kept in a sort of book-case, I believe—a book-case fitted up with pigeon-holes?'

'Yes.'

'And this receptacle stands in Mr. Lindsay's room?'

'Yes.'

'It is not kept locked?'

'No. Anyone in the office may have access to it.'

'I suppose, Mr. Beattie, papers do get lost occasionally, even in an office so well regulated as yours?'

'Oh yes.'

'And sometimes, after a long time perhaps, they turn up again?'

'Sometimes that happens, certainly.'

'It seems almost an impertinence to Mr. Lindsay to put the question, but I believe that he came to your office with high recommendations, and that until this affair his character was blameless?'

'Absolutely without reproach; and I may say that I do not for a moment believe——'

'You are not asked anything about your belief, sir,' said the Judge sternly.

Mr. Beattie fully anticipated the rebuke; but he had accomplished his purpose. He had let the jury and the whole court see that he was doing what he could for the prisoner. And yet now, for the first time, a doubt as to Beattie's integrity crossed Alec Lindsay's mind. He seemed too cool, too calm and collected, to be sincere. It looked as if he were performing a part which had been rehearsed beforehand. 'Can it be all his doing?' The thought flashed through Alec's mind only to be rejected. He could not see how Beattie could have interfered in the matter, even had he wished to do so.

Mr. Hatchett was the next witness, but he

was put into the box chiefly to give the junior counsel his turn, so that the examination of the important witness, Dr. Mackenzie, might fall to Mr. Collithorne, without a violation of the rule that senior counsel and junior shall take the witnesses alternately.

The minister was examined very minutely; the Judge's note of his evidence was as follows :

'I am a minister of the Free Church of Scotland. In the autumn of last year I came to London to see the testator, who was an old friend of mine. He declared to me his intention of leaving the sum of half a million sterling to the Church to which I belong. I did not suggest his doing so. I did not in any way urge him to do it. Nor did I disapprove of the bequest. One or two days after that, he put a paper in my hands, and told me it was the draft of his will. It was in the prisoner's handwriting. The prisoner had written to me before this, and I knew his handwriting. The bequest mentioned in it to the Free Church of Scotland was five hundred thousand pounds. It was written in words and also in figures—first in words and then in figures. That I swear.

'I was present at the execution of the will. The prisoner brought it. That is the will, so far as I can judge. I did not examine it. The prisoner read it aloud, at the testator's request. He read the bequest 'five hundred thousand pounds.' He read slowly and distinctly. I paid particular attention to that part of the will. No one was present except the testator, the prisoner, Mr. James Semple, who, I believe, is also a grand-nephew of the deceased, and myself. The servants who witnessed it did not hear it read over. The testator expressed his satisfaction with the will as it was read to him.

'When the prisoner finished reading the

will, he left the room for a short time. I believe some one called to see him. He did not take the will away with him. He left it with the deceased. I think he laid it on the bed. I did not look at it, nor touch it. When he returned the servants were called in, and the will was signed.'

As the minister ceased speaking, a sound ran round the court, as of long-drawn inspirations. Then a slight buzz of conversation arose. Every man looked at his neighbour and smiled, and then looked at the prisoner.

Alec's pale face was set, and his eyes fixed on the minister.

Sophy shuddered, and felt bewildered. She was not surprised that a girl sitting beside her whom she did not know gave a half-hysterical sob. The girl was Laura Mowbray. She was at that moment suffering something like agony. She saw that Alec was about to be condemned. She believed that her evidence might save him. Yet she dared not speak. She knew not what the consequences might be to herself, if she confessed that she had meddled with the will. She might even be accused of the fraud, and tried herself; and she shuddered at the thought.

Then Mr. Corker rose to cross-examine the witness.

'You approved of this singular bequest, Mr. Mackenzie?'

'I did not disapprove of it.'

The minister looked at the barrister disdainfully for an instant, and then turned his eyes back to the Judge, whom he had addressed throughout.

'It would have been a very fine thing for you if it had been carried out, eh?'

'The bequest was not to me.'

'Look at me, sir, and answer my questions in a straightforward manner!' shouted Mr. Corker.

Dr. Mackenzie mutely appealed to the Judge for protection; but his lordship contented himself with pointing in Mr. Corker's direction with the feather of his pen.

'I know very well the bequest was not to you; but it would have been a very good thing for you if it had been half a million instead of five thousand pounds, wouldn't it?'

'I was to be secretary to the trust,' answered the minister, after a pause.

'Exactly. For nothing, eh? Come now.'

'I could not be expected to devote a large portion of my time to work of that kind for nothing.'

'Of course not. You expected that it would be a snug little berth for you?'

The minister did not answer.

'You foresaw this when Mr. Lindsay declared his intention of making this bequest, did you not?'

'I knew that I was to be the secretary.'

'So that, so far from your coming here as a pure, impartial, disinterested witness, as my friend would have had the jury believe, you——'

Here Alec leaned over the edge of the dock, caught the speaker by his gown, and whispered something energetically into his ear.

'Nonsense!' exclaimed Mr. Corker, shaking off his client's grasp.

'Now, just listen to me, sir,' he began.

'My lord,' said Alec, 'I may say at once that Mr. Mackenzie is only telling the truth. I believe I *did* read " five hundred thousand pounds." '

There was a silence, then a murmur of astonishment.

'You had better be quiet, and leave your case to your counsel,' said the Judge in a stern voice.

Mr. Corker had indignantly thrown down his brief; but a few words from the Judge persuaded him to take it up again.

'Your lordship will excuse me for a few moments,' he said, as he turned to consult with Mr. Beattie on the change which Alec's interposition had rendered necessary in the defence.

The defence had to be altered suddenly, at the critical moment. Mr. Corker's intention had been to maintain that Mr. Lindsay had changed his mind, and had given private instructions to his nephew to prepare a will leaving only five thousand pounds to the Free Church. He had resolved to rely on Semple's evidence to neutralize, or at least to weaken, the effect produced by Dr. Mackenzie's statement. But the prisoner had just declared that Dr. Mackenzie had told the truth! It would be useless to put Semple in the box now.

'Did you ever know of such a complete idiot?' asked Mr. Corker in a whisper, as he leant over the desk before him to speak to Mr. Beattie.

'What shall we do now? We must say it was an accident—absence of mind,' whispered Beattie.

'I may say it, but the jury won't believe it for a moment. The other theory they *might* have believed.'

'You have the legal argument still.'

'Yes; but the verdict is gone. However, I suppose we must go on.'

And Mr. Corker straightened himself up and fell back into his seat, with the air of a man who has been very ill-used.

'Do you ask this witness any more questions, Mr. Corker?' asked the Judge.

'No, m' lud,' said Mr. Corker, without troubling himself to rise.

'That is the case for the prosecution, my

lord,' said Mr. Collithorne. 'Do you call any witnesses?' he added to Mr. Corker.

'No!'

'Then, may it please your lordship, gentlemen of the jury——'

'My lord, may I say a word?'

It was a woman's voice. Laura Mowbray was standing up, pale and resolute, at the back of the court.

'No; certainly not. Go on, Mr. Collithorne.'

'But I took the will myself, just before it was signed, from Mr. Lindsay's bedroom.'

Laura's good angel had triumphed. Till the last moment she had been declaring that she dared not tell what she knew—besides, it would be of no use. But in a moment, when Alec's counsel had declared that he had no witnesses, and she felt that the last moment for speech had come, she had, without deliberation, yielded to the impulse which bade her speak.

Meanwhile Mr. Collithorne and Mr. Corker were both busily disowning this disconcerting witness, and suggesting that she should not be heard. But the Judge took a different view of the matter. If anyone had touched the will, he remarked, between the time when the prisoner read it to the testator and the time when it was signed, that was clearly very important. He thought the ends of justice required that the young lady should be heard.

'I don't see that calling her can injure the defendant,' he said by way of apology to Mr. Corker.

That gentleman grunted and said nothing.

Laura was piloted to the witness-box by an usher, and in a few clear words she told how she had at Semple's request taken the will from her uncle's room, and had given it to him to read.

'Did he do anything to it, while it was in his hands?' asked the Judge.

'No.'

'And you never allowed it to go out of your sight?'

Laura hesitated.

'He took it to the window to read it, and I was standing by the door. I don't think he did anything to it. There was not time.'

'As he walked to the window, had he his side or his back to you?'

'He would have his back to me. But I don't think I was looking at him then. I don't exactly remember.'

'Well, Miss—Miss Mowbray, have you mentioned this to anyone before to-day?'

'No, my lord.'

'Why not?'

'I did not wish it to be known, if possible, that I had meddled with the will at all,' said the girl in a low voice. 'And I remember, too,' she added, 'that one night just after Mr. Lindsay died, I was at a railway-station; and I saw Mr. James Semple there, with a gentleman I do not know. And the gentleman said to him——'

But here the Judge, Mr. Collithorne, and Mr. Corker, interposed in chorus; and Laura, thoroughly disconcerted, stopped and almost burst into tears.

'That will do,' said the Judge, in a kindly tone. 'You were quite right to speak now; but you ought to have spoken sooner.'

So Laura turned away, and crept back to her seat, disappointed and humiliated. She had made the sacrifice, and all for nothing! She had been prevented telling what she considered the most important part of her story. In her agitation she had forgotten to speak of the incident of the paper which Semple had managed to obtain from his uncle's desk. But, as she reflected, she would probably not have been allowed to mention it, as she could not say that she knew it had anything to do with the will. She had expected that her testimony would cause Alec to be set at liberty. It had produced no effect whatever, beyond covering her with shame.

In this, however, she was mistaken. The Judge was eyeing the counsel, and they were eyeing him; and the thought in the minds of the three shrewd men was—'Here there was an opportunity for exchanging the will read by the prisoner for another document.'

'I think you had better go on, Mr. Collithorne,' said the Judge at length; and the Queen's Counsel was proceeding to obey, when he was interrupted for the second time.

'Let me by; I tell ye I'm a witness; let me by.'

These words, uttered in a shrill Scotch voice, were heard at one of the entrances to the court; and in another moment a queer-looking, under-sized individual, dressed in a shabby overcoat with a velvet collar, many sizes too large for him, pushed through the crowd in the passage.

'MacGowan!' exclaimed Alec involuntarily.

'Who is this?' asked the Judge testily.

'The clerk who engrossed the will, I believe, my lord,' said Mr. Collithorne, who had overheard Alec's exclamation.

'You cannot call him; you have closed your case,' said Mr. Corker to his opponent.

'But he may give evidence for the defendant, unless you object, Mr. Corker,' said the Judge.

'It's what I've come here for,' put in Mr. MacGowan.

'Really, my lord, I cannot take the responsibility of calling this witness,' said

Mr. Corker; 'I know nothing of what he may say.'

'I'm no' surprised at that,' said MacGowan, as without further invitation he stepped round to the witness-box.

'I shall take his evidence,' said the Judge, after a pause.

'Ma loard,' said MacGowan, as soon as he was sworn, 'I engrossed the wull wi' my ain haun'. The bequest to the Free Kirk was five *hunder* thoosan' pounds. So it was in the draft, an' so I wrote it in the wull, and so I read it to Maister Alexander Lindsay, when him and me compared them.

'That nicht, ma loard,' he continued, dramatically raising his right hand, 'I was refreshin' mysel' after the toils o' the day in a maist respectable public-hoose, wi' some freends, when Maister Wulliam Beattie, that is the managin' clerk at the office, cam' in and withdrew me to a private room. He telled me there had been a mistak' made, an' I would hae to copy the draft ower again; an' naething would serve him but I maun copy it ower again, then and there. I did sae, and he dictated it to me, frae the same blue draft I had had before. Only he read it *five thoosan' pounds*, leavin' oot the *hunder*.'

'Are you sure of that?' asked the Judge sharply.

'Certain sure, my lord.'

'Well?'

'Then he gied me half a sovereign and gaed awa'.'

'I leave him to you, Mr. Collithorne,' said the Judge.

'How does it happen that you immediately disappeared after this took place?' asked Mr. Collithorne.

'Weel, Messrs. Hatchett and me had a bit of difference.'

'You were dismissed, in fact?'

'Ye may ca' 't that if ye like.'

'And how was it that you have not turned up till now?'

'I have been very ill; and I only noticed to-day that the trial was coming on. If you send for my landlord he will tell ye I was in bed an' deleerious when Maister Lindsay was at the police-court.'

'You were drunk when Mr. Beattie—is that his name?—came to see you at the gin-palace, or whatever it was?'

'It is *not* a gin-palace, and I was *not* drunk. I had been drinking certainly.'

'You know perfectly well what you were about?' put in the Judge.'

'Brawly—that is, just so, my lord.'

'Hadn't we better have this Mr. Beattie in the box, and see what he says to all this,' suggested the Judge.

'Certainly, my lord. He had better be called outside. He was here a minute ago.'

But Mr. Beattie was not to be found. As soon as MacGowan's voice fell on his ears, he had realized that he had come to tell what had passed at the public-house; and he left the court by one door as his former subordinate entered by another. Taking a hansom he drove to the bank at which he kept his account, and drew out all that was due to him. Then he disappeared and was heard of no more.

The reason why Beattie had absconded was apparent to everyone in court. The plot which he had concocted was laid bare.

'I don't know whether you will think it worth while to address the jury, Mr. Collithorne,' said the Judge, after waiting some minutes. 'If the last witness is to be believed, it is plain that two wills were engrossed, in one of which the original bequest to the Free Church of Scotland was altered to five thousand pounds; and Miss

Mowbray has proved that the latter document may have been substituted for the other without the defendant's knowledge. There is nothing to show that Mr. Alexander Lindsay instigated either Beattie or MacGowan to get the second engrossment made, or that, in fact, he knew of its existence.'

'That is true, my lord; and I am altogether in your lordship's hands,' said Mr. Collithorne slowly. 'If your lordship thinks——' he paused, for the jury were putting their heads together in a significant way.

'If you would like the case to go on, gentlemen——' began the Judge; but the jurymen separated and returned to their places.

'Gentlemen of the jury, are you agreed upon your verdict?' asked the Clerk of the Arraigns.

'We are,' said the foreman.

'Do you find the prisoner at the bar guilty or not guilty?'

'Not guilty.'

Something very like a cheer broke out in the court; and the usher cried 'Silence!' with the air of a man who cared nothing for public opinion.

As for Alec, something seemed to swell in his throat, as if it would choke him; and his hand trembled as it had not trembled since his trouble had fallen on him. He looked around, and could see nothing but a sea of faces.

Then someone guided him to a little doorway in the iron railing, and helped him down the steps into the body of the court. He was a free man once more.

CHAPTER XXXIV.

AFTER THE TRIAL.

It was an embarrassing moment for Mr. Lindsay when he stepped up to his son after the acquittal was pronounced. They were both glad that a little crowd surrounded them, so that anything like conversation was impossible. Once only was the matter referred to after that day.

'I did you an injustice, Alec,' said the old man gravely; 'but the facts were sadly against you at the time.'

'No doubt they were, father,' answered his son. And nothing more was said.

It was pleasant for Alec to see the glad light in his sister's eyes; to feel the warm grasp of Blake's hand, and Cameron's grip on his shoulder; to hear Sophy Meredith's exclamation, 'I knew all along it was not your fault!' And yet, somehow, these sights and sounds seemed far away. It was almost as if he were walking in a dream, as if his real self were absent, as if he were as much alone all the time as he had been in his cell.

When the little group of friends reached the lobby of the court, they found MacGowan waiting there. He came forward, and offered Alec his hand with much affability.

'We put the snecker on him that time, eh, Maister Lindsay?' he asked, with a proud smile.

'You certainly did, MacGowan. But how was it that you did not turn up before?'

For answer MacGowan began to relate his several interviews with Beattie, which he described with great satisfaction.

'He thocht he had me, when he bade me bring the ticket for the passage, and let him see 't. But I jist waited aboot the door o' the shippin' office till a big Irishman turned up, and he agreed to lend me his ticket for ten minutes for the price of a bottle of whisky. He was waitin' roon' the corner when I gaed up to Maister Beattie, and I said I had cheinged my name for ma mither's, at which he was vastly pleased.'

'But I thought you said he saw you off,' put in Cameron.

'So he did. But I gied him the slip. I saw that before the steamer could get awa', she had to gang through the dock-gates, awa' at the tither side o' the docks. So, as she was slippin' through, I jist whummled ower the side o' the boat, an' landed on the quay. It wasna muckle o' a jump; an' as it was in the gloamin', my freen Maister Beattie never saw 't. Then I awa' to a sma' public doon by there; an' there I stoppit.'

'And drank a deal more than was good for

you, and ran through all your money, and finally took ill,' said Cameron, drawing the hero aside.

'Something like it. I kent naething aboot the hole they had pitten Maister Lindsay in, till I took up the paper the day, and saw that the trial was expeckit to come on. Ye see that big man,' he added suddenly, pointing to an official with his stave of office. 'It was fun to hear him shoutin' out, "Wull-i-am Beattie!" wi' a' his pith, when Wulliam Beattie had gien them leg-bail a quarter o' an 'oor before.'

'How did you know that?'

MacGowan glanced round before he answered, and then put his hand to his mouth, saying in a loud whisper:

'I say him slippin' awa' as I came in.'

'Why didn't you ask the Judge to have him stopped?'

'Man, did you no hear me say I owed

him a heap o' siller? He'll never fash me for that noo.'

'I doubt you're an ill stick, MacGowan,' said Cameron gravely. 'But you've done my friend a good turn this day; and I wish I could do something for ye. You just come wi' me.'

So saying, Cameron took the little man by the arm and marched him off to a neighbouring tavern, where a long and weighty consultation took place. The result of it was that the ne'er-do-weel was persuaded to emigrate, this time in earnest; and he was consigned to a second cousin of Cameron's, who had a farm in Manitoba. In his letters home MacGowan always dwells with pride upon the circumstance that he 'has been teetotal' for three or six months, as the case may be, forgetting to add that as the nearest public-house is five-and-twenty miles away, it is next to impossible for him to be anything else.

When Cameron had disappeared with Mac-Gowan, Blake carried off his friends, after giving Alec a hearty invitation to Highgate, and after expressing a hope to Mr. Lindsay that they would see him and Miss Lindsay there once more before they left town. But the old man was anxious to get back to his farm; London had no attractions for him; and he intimated his intention of going back to Scotland the next day.

As for Alec, his one desire was to find himself in his own sitting-room, alone, and at peace. That was impossible, however, for the present. He could not ignore his father and Margaret's evident expectation that he would spend the rest of the day with them. But the reunion was not in any sense a joyful one. Mr. Lindsay remembered always that he had refused to believe in his son's innocence, and had thus added to his trouble; and now it was but poor comfort to remind himself that in holding Alec to be guilty, he had only followed the dictates of his reason. Margaret, too, though she had been always loving and affectionate to her brother, knew that she had doubted him, and knew also that he had been aware of the fact. Alec tried his best to pluck up a lively if not a festive spirit at the dinner-table that evening, but he was not very successful in his efforts. His father took the opportunity of saying grace to thank the Almighty publicly that his son 'had been delivered from the snare of the fowler,' and Alec was annoyed by this open allusion to what was still a very painful theme.

To his surprise, Alec found that his father and sister had seen nothing of the sights of London during the weeks they had spent in town.

'How could we go sight-seeing, Alec, when you were in prison, and in danger?' asked Margaret, almost reproachfully.

'But you might at least have gone to Westminster Abbey and St. Paul's. You really must stay another day and see the Abbey, father. It would be almost a sin to go north again without paying it a visit.'

'As a relic of past Popery and modern prelacy,' said Mr. Lindsay, 'I think it might be well if the place were destroyed, even as the Fathers of the Reformation pulled down the abbeys and cathedrals of the north; but as a monument of antiquity the place is doubtless interesting. We will visit it tomorrow.'

'And the South Kensington Museum is also well worthy of a day's study,' said Alec.

'I am too old to care for sight-seeing, my boy.'

'If you don't care for it, Margaret would enjoy it, I am sure. Suppose you leave her behind with me, sir. She is not particularly wanted at the farm.'

'Oh, that is quite out of the question,' said Mr. Lindsay.

Alec was disposed to protest against this summary way of settling the matter, but Margaret entreated him by signs to be silent. In the course of the evening, however, a note came from Miss Lindsay to her cousin of the Castle Farm, saying that she meant to go north in two or three weeks, and would be glad if Margaret would spend the intervening time with her, and accompany her on her journey. And to this arrangement Mr. Lindsay gave a somewhat reluctant consent.

Alec did not really feel free that day, till, about ten o'clock at night, he took leave of his father and sister, and set out for his own lodgings. The air of the street was sweet to him, heavy and polluted as it was. How different the solitude of his own room from the solitude of his cell!

He had telegraphed to his landlady, and

knew that things would be in readiness. He was prepared, therefore, for the cheery glow in the window-panes; but as he opened the door he became sensible of certain familiar odours. The air was dusky with tobacco-smoke; a steaming tumbler stood on the table; and before the fire were stretched the stalwart limbs of Duncan Cameron.

'Don't say you're glad to see me, Alec, for I believe you are not,' said the visitor. 'I've been here for the last three hours. I might have kenned that your friends would lay hold on ye, body and soul.'

'You know very well I'm glad to see you, Duncan.'

'I don't believe you. You might have been pleased to see me three hours ago. But there are times when a lee is more or less excusable. Such a time is the present.'

'Have you dined?'

'Eight hours ago.'

'Have you supped?'

'Not particularly.'

'We'll have some supper at once, then; and you will stay for the night.'

This was settled; and after supper came pipes and tumblers, seasoned with scraps of information about old College cronies—memories which, though only a few years old, seemed to the two young men to lie already far behind them—and a due proportion of metaphysics.

In the middle of the talk Cameron rose, and pulling a short instrument from his pocket, begged Alec to unbutton his waistcoat.

'What are you going to do?'

'Satisfy my curiosity.'

'You don't mean that there is anything the matter with me?'

'That is what I want to find out.'

'There is no actual disease,' said Cameron,

when his examination was concluded. 'The pulmonary organs are sound, but they are far from strong. You must take care of yourself for some time. Those weeks in confinement have injured you more than you think.'

Then Cameron lit his pipe for the fourth time, and smoked awhile in silence.

'Duncan, what is your religion now?' asked Alec suddenly.

'*Religio medici;* that is, none at all.'

'I'm sorry to hear you say that,' said Alec gravely. 'But I don't believe you.'

'I was thinking of definite faith, of dogmas,' said Cameron. 'Of course I have religious instincts, emotions, and so on; but I can't classify them.'

'"True religion consisteth in great part in the affections," says Jonathan Edwards. Perhaps you think dogmas are hindrances, not helps.'

'True houses consist in great part of walls,' retorted the Highlander; ' is that to say they should have no foundations ?'

' But I thought you said you had no dogmas.'

' Exactly ; and therefore I don't profess to have any religion. It makes me sick,' he continued, getting up and walking about the room, ' to hear the way in which men prate about " the fetters of dogma" and so on. I hate phrases that beg the question like that. Good heavens, man !' he went on, turning upon Alec with a frown, as if he had been personally ill-used or insulted, ' canna the moles see that it a' depends on whether the dogma's *true* or no ? If it's not true, it may be a " fetter," no doubt. But if it's true, what can it be but a heaven-sent boon ? You might as well talk o' releasin' the earth from the fetter that binds it to the sun. That would be a fine result o' the freethinker's theory carried out in practice.'

'But I thought——'

'Look at my own subject,' continued Cameron, not heeding his companion. 'Take anatomy. If you have false opinions on the subject printed and promulgated, they will no doubt do harm. But if certain opinions are indisputably true——'

'That is just what is denied.'

'Then what is the sense of begging the question by assuming that they are false?'

'Then you do believe in dogma in religion?'

'No religion can exist without dogmas, be they many or few, any more than a tub can exist without a bottom. But whether the dogmas of Christianity are *true* is more than I can say.'

'But there must be a God?'

'That's just what I don't feel sure about,' said Cameron slowly. 'Why may not matter be eternal, and produce of itself all we know of?'

'Because, for one thing, the chances against its being in a position to produce anything at all were millions to one.'

'That is true. But then, how can we tell that under other conditions of temperature, and so forth, other results, totally different, but equally wonderful, might not have followed?'

'All to come out of so many metals and gases?' asked Alec. 'I think the man who believes *that* must be the most credulous of mortals.'

'I didn't say I believed it, did I?'

'Then there's the conscience, and the moral law within.'

'Inherited instincts,' murmured Cameron.

'That won't do; I tell you it won't do,' said Alec firmly. 'There are virtues that are highly prized nowadays which never could have come into existence, much less have lived and flourished, if they had been dependent on those principles alone. Take humility, the power of self-sacrifice, kindness to the sick, to the aged, to dumb animals, and so on. Self-sacrifice does not naturally tend to the survival of the fittest, say what you like. Do stags become less fit to survive because they butt a wounded deer out of the herd, or leave it to die of starvation? Why should men who nurse the sick and tend the aged become stronger than those who do not?'

'There's sense in what you say, Alec; and of course, if we find a fact that natural principles won't explain, and religious principles will explain, that is a great matter. But I'm going to turn in. Good-night.'

'Seems to me you have first of all got to explain how the natural principles themselves came here,' said Alec, as a parting shot at his friend.

Cameron was forced to leave London on the following day, so that it was impossible for him to accompany the party that was going to visit the Abbey, as Alec wished him to do. His feeling was that Duncan would help him to entertain his father. But Alec soon saw that his father needed no entertaining. From the moment when the old man's eyes fell on the pile, standing like a heavenly temple reared by angel hands among the haunts of men, he neither spoke nor listened to what was said to him. All his faculties were absorbed in admiration. He walked slowly round and round, now letting his eye wander at will in the maze of delicate, lace-like tracery, now stepping back that he might the more fairly grasp the proportions of the building.

It was with difficulty that Alec managed to draw him inside; and when he raised his eyes to the forest of columns and arches, the glades of open stonework, with lanes of light between, whose beauty spoke as with silver chimes to the listening heart, the old man sank down upon one of the benches, overpowered with wonder and delight. His son and daughter left him there, and went to make a tour of the chapels. When they returned he was still sitting where they had left him, rapt in admiration.

'Don't you think it would be better without all those statues?' whispered Margaret to her father.

'You don't need to look at them!' said the old man, almost impatiently, as he let his eyes once more travel slowly upwards to the dim recesses of the roof.

'Shall I remind father of what he said last night about the Fathers of the Reformation and the Scotch abbeys?' whispered Alec to his sister.

'Oh, I entreat you not to speak of that! It would be a shame to throw that in his teeth. He would most likely be very angry; and it would spoil all his pleasure,' said Margaret.

Mr. Lindsay was persuaded to make the round of the chapels, and to visit Livingstone's grave, and the coronation-stone. But even the matchless beauties of the Lady Chapel could not detain him long from the spot at which he could see aisle and nave, choir and transept, unite to form one glorious whole.

Next day, Mr. Lindsay left London for his own home; and Margaret went to stay with Miss Lindsay at Claremont Gardens. As a matter of course Alec was there pretty often, for the short time that his sister was to be in town.

On one occasion when he called only Laura was at home. It was the first time they had been alone together since the day of the trial.

'I have never thanked you yet, Laura,' said Alec, 'for what you did for me at the court. Every day I have hoped for the chance of speaking to you alone; but I have not had an opportunity until now.'

Laura blushed almost painfully. She was sitting on a low seat near the fire, while Alec stood at the other end of the hearth-rug, with his elbow on the mantelpiece, leaning his head on his hand, and looking, not at his companion, but at the fire smouldering in the grate.

'It was very brave of you, and very, very good of you.' He stopped suddenly. He could not remind her that the special merit of her giving evidence was the fact that she had brought discredit on herself in doing so.

'It was only what I ought to have done; but I should have done it sooner.'

'I am very glad you did not,' said Alec quickly. 'It was fortunate for me that you said nothing to the lawyers who were defending me. They would probably have prevented you from speaking in court at all.'

'I had hoped that I—that what I told might have done you some good,' said Laura, almost bitterly. 'It did no good at all.'

'Indeed, you are mistaken!'

'It was the evidence of that queer Scotch clerk that set you free.'

'No; it was yours. Or rather, you and he together secured the acquittal. You added the missing link in the chain.'

'Then I am well repaid.'

'And I shall be grateful to you as long as I live.'

But Laura was not satisfied with this. If he would only turn and look at her! But he stood there, gazing at the red embers without seeing them.

'Surely,' thought Laura, 'he has not ceased to love me? He is not one who easily forgets.'

'Won't you sit down?' she said gently. But he did not seem to hear her. She was determined that he should speak.

'Miss Lindsay is going north sooner than she intended,' she said, almost sharply.

'Ah!'

'Yes. I leave for Brighton the day after to-morrow.'

'I am sorry you are going. You are to live with some relations of your own, are you not?'

'Yes; with some distant relations of my mother's. I am sure I shall dislike them.'

'Don't say that.'

'Why not? I don't suppose you care very much what sort of life I lead.'

For answer, Alec turned and met her glance. There was a gentle reproach in his look; but he said nothing.

'It is too late,' said Laura to herself. 'He does not care for me now.'

'I, at least, am glad to think that you will be rich,' said she aloud.

'I? I shall have about five thousand pounds, I believe.'

'But I was told that the half-million would

not go to the Free Church—that it would be divided between you and your cousin.'

'Surely you do not think I could take it?'

The girl stared at him without saying a word.

'It does not belong to me. My uncle never meant that I should have it. I have no more right to that money, morally, than you have.'

'And you mean that you will give it up!' ejaculated Laura.

'What else could I do? If you said to me, "Give that sovereign to the Archbishop of Canterbury, and keep that shilling for yourself." And if by mistake you gave me the shilling instead of the sovereign, and the sovereign for the shilling, would I be entitled to keep the sovereign and hand over the shilling? You can't say you think so for a moment.'

'I think you are mad to hand over such an enormous sum to those Presbyterians; and any sensible person would say just the same.'

'But you cannot understand. My uncle intended——'

'I don't care what your uncle intended. If he did, or meant to do, an insane thing, that is no reason why you should do one too.'

'Do you really think it would be honest to keep that money, when it never was intended for me?' asked Alec slowly.

'It matters very little what I think, for I know very well you won't listen to me. But I suppose what the law gives you is your own, and if you give it away, it will be your own act, and, to my mind, a very foolish one.'

'I have written to the executors of the will, saying that I would only take my share of any residue there may be after the half-million is deducted.'

'Oh! Well, I suppose there is no more to be said.'

Alec was silent for a minute. Then he started up.

'I am going now. I won't wait for my aunt and Margaret.'

Laura rose and gave him her hand.

'Don't think I am angry with you,' she said, with one of her old bright smiles. 'I have no business to be, in any case.'

'I am sure, if you think it over, you will see that I could do nothing else. Good-bye.'

'Good-bye.'

There was so much he would have liked to say. It seemed so cold, so ungrateful, to part with a conventional 'Good-bye,' without a word of the past, without a word of the future. But the thoughts in his heart could not be spoken. It was almost as if he had been watching for an hour beside the grave of one whom he had loved.

And Laura was sitting in her old attitude over the fire, struggling hard to keep back her tears.

'I will not cry for him; I will not,' she said to herself. 'He is not worth it. He is a perfect fool. To fling away all that money! And we might have been so happy! I could not marry a man so poor as he is now; but he might have asked me, all the same. Well,' and here the poor girl gave a long-drawn sigh, 'I shall never like anyone else half so well.'

CHAPTER XXXV.

MISS MEREDITH INSISTS ON BEING OBEYED.

It was not until his sister and aunt had left London that Alec Lindsay began to feel the effect of his imprisonment and of the anxiety he had suffered. His natural energy had vanished. He was content to hang all day over the fire, and began to have a morbid shrinking from intercourse with strangers. He fancied that the shadow of the accusation yet clung to him. His cough had never left him; and he felt more and more indisposed for exertion of any kind. He lived quite alone, often spending whole days without exchanging a word with any human being. The arrangement with Messrs. Hatchett,

Small, and Hatchett had been tacitly abandoned; and he had not been able to decide on taking any fresh step. There was little wonder that, living as he did, he became gloomy and melancholy, tired of his life and of everything around him.

One afternoon he was surprised by a visit from Hubert Blake.

'My dear fellow, what is the matter with you?' were Blake's first words.

'Nothing, so far as I know.'

'You look like a ghost.'

'Nonsense.'

'You may call it nonsense if you like, but it is true. What are you doing with yourself now?'

'Nothing in particular. A prolonged fit of laziness.'

'I doubt if it is laziness. Do you live here all alone, without any regular occupation?'

'I go to the British Museum and read sometimes.'

There was a pause of a minute or two, and then Blake said gravely:

'You are not yourself, Alec. You used to be full of energy and spirits. What has happened to you?'

'Nothing whatever. Please don't go on like that.'

'I'm afraid you were harder hit two months ago than we supposed. A man can't come through an experience of that kind without paying for it.'

Alec's thin face flushed painfully. Blake saw that his friend wished to be let alone; but he could not help thinking that anything was better for him than the melancholy into which he seemed to be sinking.

'You should not live so much alone,' he began again.

'There are very few men I would care

to live with. I don't see what else I can do.'

'I should take a change — go into the country.'

'That would not mend matters.'

'Or travel.'

'Too much bother.'

'But you can't go on like this.'

'Why not? Blake, you are very good, but you may as well let me alone. To tell the truth, I don't care much what happens. I feel as if my life were ended. I don't consider,' he went on, speaking rapidly, as if he were anxious to finish what he had to say, 'that my name can ever be cleared of the taint of the Old Bailey. I fancy men look askance at me. I have no desire to begin life again. My ambitions are dead, and I don't want them to come to life again. What does it matter?'

'All this simply means that you are run

down, out of sorts,' said Blake, rising to his feet. 'You should take a long voyage.'

Alec shook his head.

'At least, come and dine with us at Highgate to-morrow. I have something to tell you.'

'Much obliged, Blake; but I'd rather not.'

'I do think you might exert yourself as far as that goes,' said Hubert; but seeing that Alec was very unwilling to go, he dropped the subject, and soon afterwards left him.

In a day or two, however, Alec received a note from Sophy Meredith, repeating the invitation in such terms that he found it impossible to decline it; and accordingly, a few days afterwards he found himself once more at Caen House, Highgate.

The master of the house was not present at dinner. It was a late, cold spring; and Mr.

Blake found it better to confine himself to his own room. Nothing of importance was said at the dinner-table; but Alec fancied that his hostess seemed brighter and franker than usual, and once or twice he observed a glance passing between her and his friend which he did not quite understand.

When the little party returned to the drawing-room, Miss Elmwood at once settled herself comfortably in an easy-chair by the fire, and Sophy went over to the piano. Blake went up to her to help her to choose some music; and Alec, who was sitting close by, was surprised to see Sophy lay her hand in a familiar way on his friend's arm, looking into his face with a bright smile as she did so. The next instant she caught Alec's look, and, blushing deeply, she turned to Blake and whispered :

'Did you not tell Mr. Lindsay that we are engaged?'

'No,' he whispered in reply. 'The fact is, the poor fellow looked so wretched, in mind as well as in body, that I did not like the idea of flaunting my happiness in his face. But go on playing, and I will tell him now.'

Sophy did as she was bid, but her performance had a good many slips in it. Meantime Blake had seated himself beside Alec, and answering his look, said:

'Yes; Miss Meredith and I have been engaged about a week.'

'Why didn't you tell me when you came to see me the other day? But I beg your pardon; I have no business to ask questions like that.'

'Not at all, my dear fellow. I—the fact is——'

'Surely you did not think I would grudge you your good fortune, or envy you?'

'Not that, certainly; and yet you seemed

so depressed that I did not care to allude to the subject.'

'It is a comfort to know that there is some happiness yet in the world. Sometimes it seems to me there is very little of it left. And I am sure few people deserve a share of it better than you and Miss Meredith.'

'Don't say that of me, Alec. It is very far from the truth.'

'I wish you joy with all my heart.'

'You, too, have had your little romance. I remember, at least, that when we were at Loch Long——'

'That is all over,' said Alec quietly, but there was a sad, wistful look in his face. Presently he found an opportunity of congratulating Sophy on her engagement.

'Thank you, Mr. Lindsay. But, do you know, I have something on my mind to say to you. I do hope you won't be offended if I say it.'

'That means you are going to lecture me.'

'Oh no!'

'Only a spoonful of jam? I fear the pill is there all the same.'

'Do you know that is the first thing I have heard you say in your old manner for months. You are not well. I see it plainly. You are very far from well.'

'Which is a polite way of saying that I am lazy, moody, and so on, and that I should shake off my melancholy, and set to work at something. I feel I ought to do that; but, to tell the truth, I feel as if I hadn't the spirit to attempt it.'

'It seems to me that you are slipping the medicine into the spoon yourself; and besides, the dose you have chosen is one that doesn't suit your complaint. It is the weak state of health you are in which is to blame. Now, I want you to go and see a doctor.'

'I assure you, Miss Meredith, it is quite

unnecessary. There is very little, if anything, the matter with me.'

'Let us say it is unnecessary. Won't you take the trouble of going, if I ask you?'

'Certainly.'

'Then I do ask you.'

That, of course, settled the matter; and before Alec left the house Miss Meredith gave him the name and address of the doctor she wished him to consult.

The following morning, accordingly, Alec spent in the physician's waiting-room. The room was nearly full when he entered it; and as most of those present had made appointments beforehand with the doctor, and were consequently preferred, he had more than an hour to wait. There was plenty of time for him to observe his fellow-patients. One little group, in particular, arrested his attention. It consisted of a young man, a few years older than himself, a girl who was evidently his wife, and a child, a merry little fellow about three years old. The young mother was evidently the patient. She was thin and hollow-eyed; the colour came and went in her pallid cheeks, and her cough was sometimes painful to listen to. The husband sat moodily staring before him. The mother busied herself with the child.

As it happened, the boy took a strong fancy for Alec's stick; and after a shy smile and a faint excuse from his mother, the child succeeded in attaining his object. This led to the interchange of a few remarks between Alec and the child's parents, from which it appeared that the young man was a clerk in some mercantile house in the City, and was spending an unexpected holiday in the effort to ascertain exactly what ailed his wife. To Alec it seemed plain that the girl (for she seemed hardly beyond girlhood) was in consumption. The only question was what progress the disease had made.

When it was Alec's turn to enter the consulting-room, he thought that the doctor made a ridiculously minute examination, and asked him a number of very unnecessary questions. But he changed his mind when the physician pronounced his verdict. The substance of it was that Alec was in a very precarious state of health; that his lungs were exceedingly delicate, and that he was predisposed to consumption. The prescription was change of scene and cheerful society in the meantime, and a voyage to Australia or a winter spent in Egypt.

'I see you are tempted to make light of the matter,' said the doctor. 'All I can say is, that if you go on as you are doing now, you will not be alive this day twelve months. You had better get one or two of your relations to take a trip to Ventnor with you. Don't go alone. Good-afternoon.'

Alec was startled by what he was told;

and yet, so deep was his melancholy that he was conscious of a certain satisfaction in being able to think of his death as an event that was possibly not far off.

He had left the house and had gone some little distance before he noticed that he had taken a wrong turning, and would be forced to retrace his steps. He had gone back nearly as far as the doctor's house, when he met the young couple whom he had noticed in the waiting-room.

Alec was startled by the fierce look in the husband's face. It was the face of a desperate man. He was striding on, apparently without thinking where he was going, dragging his child carelessly by the hand, while his staring eyes and clenched teeth told of the storm that was raging within. His wife trudged on by his side in silence, pale to the lips, with a scared look in her face. Moved by some impulse, Alec stopped right in front of them, and, without any formal apology, asked at once :

'What did the doctor say ?'

'What did he say? Death. That's what he said. It may be in a year, or it may be in three months. My God !'

The humble City clerk was transformed by misery into something like a madman. He gripped his wife by the arm, as if he would defy Death himself to tear her from his side.

'She's all I have, and I can't live without her. I can't, and I won't.'

Alec shuddered, but he could not meet the man's eyes, and dropped his own before them.

'And the children ; what is to become of them ?'

'Come, Tom ; come home with me,' said his wife gently, as she tried to release her husband's tightening grasp.

But he did not hear her.

'Ay ; and the doctor says, if she could go

to Egypt for a time, or the south of France, her life would be spared. Egypt! Or the south of France! For a year, he says. Oh yes, it would save her life. That's the good of being rich, you see. You can buy your wife's life.'

'What is your name? Where do you live?' said Alec.

'What have you to do with that?'

'Hush, Tom!' put in the girl at his side. 'And do let go my arm, you hold me so tight. Tell the gentleman where we live. He won't do us any harm.'

But the man, suddenly dropping his wife's arm, strode on without saying another word.

'Tell me the name of your husband's employers; he said he was a clerk in the City,' said Alec to the girl, walking on by her side.

'Cole and Fletcher, sir. They're tea merchants in Devizes Street.'

'And your name is?'

'Hardy, sir.'

'Thank you. Good-day.'

There was sympathy in Alec's face, if there was none in his language; and as he slowly walked homewards he asked himself, 'Why should I not do it? I have all I need; more, probably, than I shall ever wish to use. Of course it is a risk; but I don't think I could do better.'

And next morning Thomas Hardy received a short note, which enclosed a cheque for three hundred pounds, signed 'Alexander Lindsay.'

CHAPTER XXXVI.

SICK UNTO DEATH.

It was a wet, cheerless day in the end of March. The rain fell without ceasing, and the air was bitterly cold. There was not a sign of spring in field or hedgerow; and here and there, in the furrows and in sheltered spots where the wind could not penetrate, the snow still lingered.

Alec Lindsay was seated in the battered old coach, being conveyed to the Castle Farm. He had determined to see if his native air would restore him to health. For he could no longer persuade himself that there was little or nothing the matter with him. He felt weaker every day. The preparations for leaving London and the long journey had tired him excessively; and now his one desire was for rest.

As the lumbering vehicle approached the well-remembered corner, he saw the dog-cart waiting. His father was driving it; and the old man was startled when he saw his son's face, and still more when he took his hand.

'You are far from well, Alec,' said the laird.

'I am tired. I shall be better to-morrow,' said he, getting into the dog-cart.

'I think we had better stop at Dr. Henderson's, and ask him to come over and see you to-morrow.'

'Oh dear me, no,' said Alec, in an irritated tone. 'I only want a good night's rest.'

But on the following morning he did not come down to breakfast. He had caught a cold on the journey, and he complained of a pain in his side. Dr. Henderson was sent for, and when he saw his patient he looked very grave.

'Inflammation of the lungs,' he said to Mr. Lindsay, when he went downstairs.

'But there is no danger, is there?' asked the old laird, with alarm in his eyes.

'I would not like to say there's no danger,' said the doctor cautiously. 'He's young, and I hope he'll win through; but he seems very listless and careless about himself. That's a bad sign.'

'You'll do all that can be done, I'm sure, doctor; but if you think further advice desirable, you'll not spare expense.'

'A' the doctors in Europe could do no more than I'm doing,' said the doctor testily. 'I'll come round the morn. He may be easier then, but I doubt no. We must have patience.'

Margaret nursed her brother with great

skill and tenderness. She was born to be a nurse; and her habitual self-repression made it easy for her to conceal the anxiety she was feeling.

It was impossible for her to be always in the sick-room, and Alec liked best to be left alone. It was the room that had always been his own. Here he had read and worked to prepare himself for College. At that old-fashioned window he had often sat, dreaming dreams which would never come true. How fair the world had seemed to him but a few short years before! How delightful the battle when he would match himself against his fellows, against men born with greater advantages than his own, and in which he would come off victorious, winning not only wealth but honourable renown! And he had succeeded in nothing. It was only by an accident, he told himself, that he was not now sitting in a convict's cell, or lying on a pallet in some prison infirmary. That he had escaped; but he had learned, or thought he had learned, that the prizes he had set his heart on were not worth winning. The whole world did not seem to him to hold anything worthy of the devotion of a lifetime. All this passed through his mind continually, in spite of the pain, but in a confused way, as if he had thought it all out and had wearied of it long ago.

On the third day the doctor looked very grave, and said he would come again in the evening.

'You think my son is worse, then?' said Mr. Lindsay.

The doctor paused for a moment.

'We must hope for the best,' he said at last.

A chill struck to the father's heart. Was it possible that this boy, of whom in secret he had been so proud, the only hope of his house, was to die? Inwardly he trembled, but outwardly he was as composed as ever.

'Do you think,' he said slowly, 'that he ought to be told?'

'I think you might ask him if there is any friend he would like to see,' said the doctor. 'That will make him understand.'

When the doctor left him, the laird sat down in a kind of stupor. He could not believe it. Was he, an old man, not far from the grave, to live, while death seized his strong, bright-eyed boy? He shivered; and as he sat there alone he realized that the bereavement would be worse to him than it need have been. He had shown the lad but little of a father's tenderness, little even of the tenderness which he actually felt. Alec had never confided in him, and he had resented the want of confidence. But he had never tried to see things from the boy's standpoint; he had never made allowances for him, never yielded to him, never tried to sympathize with his plans. He had wished his son to be as himself. That could not be; and he had never acquiesced in the decree of nature which had given the young man other standards, other ideas, other aims, than his own. And now the end was come.

He could not bring himself as yet to go upstairs and tell his son the truth. But Alec had already learned it.

'Maggie,' he said suddenly. 'Does the doctor think I will get better?'

Margaret stepped back so that her brother could not see her face, and steadied her voice before she answered:

'He hopes you will. You have a splendid constitution, he says.'

'But there is a chance that I may not?'

Margaret could not speak. She would have broken down, and she was determined not to do that. On her brother's face was a look of satisfaction, as of one who heard that a long-expected haven was in sight. Then that expression passed away, and was succeeded by a wandering, troubled gaze.

'I would like to see Duncan Cameron,' Alec whispered. 'Do you think my father would send for him?'

'I am sure he would, dear; I will go and ask him now,' said Margaret, as she kissed her brother and softly left the room.

Mr. Lindsay was not well pleased to hear of Alec's wish.

'It is a stranger he wishes to be with him at the last,' he said to himself bitterly.

But he set off himself to walk the five miles which lay between the farm and the nearest telegraph office.

That evening Duncan Cameron was at the farm. Little was said between the two; but Alec seemed to find comfort in his friend's presence. In a short time Mr. Lindsay beckoned Cameron out of the room.

'You are a doctor,' said the old man, in a hard, constrained voice. 'What do you think? Is he likely to recover?'

'I cannot say,' said Cameron. 'He is very ill, and very weak. If he were a patient of my own, or a stranger——'

'Yes?'

'I should fear that he would not live through the night.'

The old man turned away without a word, went to his own room, and threw himself on his knees at the side of his bed. He could not pray. But under his breath he whispered:

'Oh, my son, would God I could die for thee! Oh, Alec, my son, my son!'

And the tears ran unbidden down his withered, weather-beaten cheeks.

Meantime Cameron had gone back to the

sick-room, and there he sat down to watch by his friend, while Margaret rested.

'Cameron,' said Alec, speaking slowly and with pain, 'when I am gone they may put on my tombstone, "Born a man, died a failure."'

'Hold your tongue, man.'

'I have been a failure in everything I ever tried,' whispered Alec. 'I wonder why I was born—it seems to have been such a useless existence.'

'You say that, and you believe in a God!' exclaimed Cameron. 'If you don't, you may talk about useless existences, and so forth. But if you believe in a God, you must believe that there is a reason, and a good reason, for everything, whether you see it or not. If there is a God, and God determined to make you, it was better that you should live. And if you failed, it is better that you should fail, because if God had wished you to succeed, He might easily have brought that about, I suppose?'

'Yes, it must be so. There is comfort in that.'

'Of course there is. There is more than comfort in it. There is everything in it. And yet men go on saying they believe in God, and grumbling at every stone they strike their foot against.'

A long pause followed.

Alec was hardly able to speak, but a faint smile crossed his face.

'You are always the same, Cameron.'

'And if you talk any more I will leave the house this instant. If you have any peace in your mind, keep it, and thank God. But don't say another syllable, unless you want to kill yourself.'

All through that night Cameron and Margaret watched by turns.

About four in the morning Cameron touched

the bell which stood at the side of the bed; and in a few seconds Margaret was in the room. Alec was sitting upright, supported by his friend's arms and breast, while he laboured and gasped for breath.

'Call his father,' whispered Cameron.

Margaret longed to fly to her brother's side; but she did as she was told, and soon the old man obeyed the summons.

'It cannot last much longer,' whispered Cameron to Margaret, as she stood sobbing at his side.

The three stood there and waited helplessly while the life and death struggle went on. At last the breathing became more regular, and Alec was able to look at the faces of those around him.

'I think you had better go now; it only excites him to see so many of us here,' said Cameron, still speaking in a whisper. 'I will call you again if he should get worse, but I don't think it will be necessary. I think he will do now.'

Cameron was right. Alec had youth and a magnificent constitution on his side; and from that night he grew gradually better.

* * * * *

The sun was shining bright and strong through the little square windows of the parlour, when the invalid came down for the first time after his illness. It was May; the rain was over and gone, and the time of the singing of birds had come. Alec's heart sang with them, he hardly knew why. It was partly the reaction of a young and vigorous system after the illness and the mental depression through which he had passed; but he had undergone another change of which he said nothing. He no longer looked on the world as an arena in which success meant all that was worth living for, and failure irretrievable disaster.

During his convalescence there had been some talk of the future, and it had been settled that in order to get rid of the weakness in his lungs Alec should spend one or two years in a dry, warm climate. Cameron had recommended a voyage to Australia; and finally it was settled that the invalid should wait at the Castle Farm till he was quite fit to travel, and then sail for Melbourne. If he found that the climate suited him, he was to settle down for a year or more, and learn sheep-farming.

In view of so long a parting, he was in no hurry to leave home; and for the first time since his boyhood he enjoyed staying at the farm.

'Alec,' said his father to him one day, not long before the time fixed for his departure, 'did I ever tell you that I had heard from your cousin Semple?'

'No!' exclaimed Alec in great **astonish-**

ment. 'When? Where is he? What is he doing?'

'It was during your illness, so of course I did not mention it to you. He was in Spain —in hiding. He was miserably poor; in fact, he wrote begging me to send him money, if it were only a few shillings.'

'Have you his letter?'

'I burned it.'

'And did you——'

'Send him money? No, indeed! Was it likely? His punishment is nothing comparatively. But it is written, "Vengeance is Mine."'

There was an air of decided satisfaction in the old man's manner as he quoted the text.

'Do you remember the address?' asked Alec, after a pause.

'No,' said Mr. Lindsay shortly.

'It is very strange to hear of his being in poverty,' said Alec, 'when he is entitled to so much wealth. I heard before I left London that the trustees of the Free Kirk could not hope to succeed in getting the half-million from a court of law.'

'So it has been decided; but Semple is afraid to come forward and claim the money. He fears he may be prosecuted, and, for anything he knows, sent to penal servitude.'

'Perhaps he does not even know that in spite of the trick he played he is entitled to half the residue of the estate.'

'I dare say he does not.'

'I wonder what he is doing now.'

'He won't starve,' said Mr. Lindsay calmly. 'He will manage to exist somehow till he thinks the worst danger is past, and then we shall hear of his trying to get hold of the money.'

'Did you think I did right in renouncing my share of it?' said Alec, after a pause.

'You did not consult me at the time,' said

the old man stiffly; 'and there is little use in speaking of it now.'

'You see, my uncle never intended for one moment that I should get two hundred and fifty thousand pounds of his money. I felt that I could not honestly take it.'

'No doubt. Have you fixed whether you will go by the *Queen of the South* or the *Glenstrae?*'

From which Alec understood that his father would have agreed with Laura Mowbray in thinking that he was not morally bound to carry out his uncle's wishes.

'Conscience must be obeyed, no doubt,' said the old man, suddenly returning to the subject. 'But in important matters it is well to take time for due deliberation, and to consult those whose opinion is entitled to respect.'

'I am afraid, sir, I could hardly have expected a Free Kirk minister to advise me to retain the money,' said Alec maliciously. 'If I had had recourse to an Established Church pastor, he might perhaps have seen the matter in a different light.'

Then, seeing that his father looked nettled, Alec hastily began to speak of something else.

It was the middle of summer before the time of parting came. The *Glenstrae* (the ship which had been chosen) sailed from the Clyde; and Alec's father and sister, as well as his friend Cameron, went down to Greenock where the vessel was lying, to see him on board.

The separation was painful, but it was, after all, so different from that other parting which a few weeks before had seemed so near at hand! The last hand-shakes were exchanged; and Alec's friends stepped on board the tug which was to convey them back to the shore. He saw them land; he saw his father's tall, bent form, with Margaret at his side, standing motionless at the edge of the quay. He watched them until it was no longer possible to see the signals they made, till their forms were lost in the distance. A few minutes afterwards he begged a fellow-passenger for the loan of a field-glass which was lying beside him, that he might have a nearer look at the land he was leaving. And happening to turn the glass upon the wharf, he saw that Margaret and his father were standing there still.

CHAPTER XXXVII.

THE FUGITIVE'S RETURN.

BEFORE Miss Lindsay left London she accompanied her late cousin's ward to Victoria, and saw her depart for Brighton. The old lady was by no means sorry that this was the last she was to see of Laura Mowbray. There had been from the first hour of their meeting a natural antipathy between the two women. Miss Lindsay's ruling idea was that of duty, while Laura's chief aim in life was to get as much amusement, or, failing that, as much comfort as possible, out of her existence. They had put up with each other because they happened to be members of the same household, and each had too much sense to indulge in quarrelling or recrimination. Naturally they both felt it to be a relief when the connection came to an end.

But no sooner were Miss Lindsay and Margaret seated in the carriage which conveyed them back to Claremont Gardens, than the old lady's conscience began to trouble her. It told her that she had done nothing for the girl who had been for some years in a manner under her care. She had not tried to wean her from her pleasure-loving, selfish habits. She had not tried to sympathize with her, or to make life in Mr. Lindsay's house, which was often cheerless enough, a whit more pleasant for her. Beyond lending volumes of sermons and religious memoirs to her to read on Sundays, she had not tried to influence the motherless girl for good. Why had she not thought of all this before it was too late?

'It was with a sigh, therefore, that she turned to Margaret, and said :

'Poor lassie! I wish she may do weel.'

'I think few people are better able to take care of themselves than Miss Mowbray,' responded Margaret.

'I think Alec was greatly taken with her some time back,' said Miss Lindsay, after a pause.

'She encouraged both him and that wretch, James Semple,' said Margaret, with more vehemence than was usual with her; 'and I believe she meant to take the one that turned out to be Uncle James's heir. She has no principle. I believe she would marry anyone who was rich enough to give her all the comforts of life and take her to plenty of balls and parties.'

'It doesna become you to speak ill o' the lassie as soon as her back's turned,' said Miss Lindsay; and to this rebuke Margaret vouchsafed no reply.

Meanwhile Laura was trying to realize that

once more a great change had come into her life. The comfortable, monotonous life of Mr. Lindsay's house was already for her a thing of the past. What the future had in store for her she had no means of guessing. A cousin of her mother's, who had married a Mr. Crosby, had offered her a home, and she had accepted the offer. Of Mr. Crosby she only knew that he was a coal merchant, and that he lived at Richmond Villa, Brighton. He might be a poor man, or he might be well-to-do; though from the fact that Mrs. Crosby had accepted Laura's proposal to pay her sixty pounds a year for her board and lodging, it might be supposed that the Crosbys were not rich.

'Whatever they are like,' said Laura to herself, 'my life can't be more dull with them than it has been for the last three years. And if I don't like them, I can always go away again.'

But fate had decreed that in both of these points Laura was to be disappointed.

The girl's heart sank within her as the cab stopped at 'Richmond Villa,' which was, in fact, nothing more than a shabby, stucco-fronted cottage. The crying of a baby reached her ears before she had time to raise the knocker; and no sooner had she done so than she became conscious that two dirty children were peering at her from the window at her left hand.

Mrs. Crosby was a large, flabby, good-natured woman, who seemed incapable of being injuriously affected by any domestic troubles whatever. She was always in a muddle, always undecided, always unpresentable in appearance, and always contented. Her husband, on the contrary, was a little, sharp-eyed, foxy-haired man with a rasping, disagreeable voice, and an uncertain temper. Each of them had, without knowing it, drawn a prize in the lottery of marriage. Either Mr. or Mrs. Crosby would have driven any other man or woman mad in a week; but they got on together tolerably well.

'You are very welcome, Miss Mowbray,' he said to Laura that evening, 'if you can put up with the discomfort of this house. I'm used to it, and I don't mind; but with you it may be different.'

Laura did not know what to say in answer to this speech; but Mrs. Crosby remarked with the utmost composure:

'Law, Mr. Crosby, how can you say so? I'm sure everything's very comfortable, though at present a little unsettled. But you must never mind Mr. Crosby, my dear. All men grumble and find fault; and if you just let them alone, it never does anyone any harm.'

Life at Richmond Villa was certainly uneventful; but very much to her own surprise Laura found that it interested her. It was the first time she had ever formed one of a family circle; and though the children were by no means attractive, they amused her, and pleased her by coming to her with their little wants and cares, their joys and sorrows.

And before Laura had been long enough in the house to decide whether it would not be better to leave it and go and live by herself in a boarding-house, an event happened which settled the question for her. The Patent Match-box Company, whose shares she had bought on her lawyer's advice at twenty per cent. premium, went into liquidation; and after a miserable period of anxiety Laura found that only nine hundred pounds of her money could be saved out of the wreck. She was thankful to remain with Mrs. Crosby as nursery-governess. It was a hard, dull life; but the very hardness and dulness of it did the girl good. She was forced to think of other things than her own amusement and her own pleasure. Almost insensibly she grew less self-indulgent, more considerate for others, more simple and straightforward.

One day, about six months after Laura had first come to Brighton, she was returning home, late in the afternoon, when she was stopped by a man whom she took for a beggar. As she was searching her pocket for a copper, he spoke to her.

'Laura—Miss Mowbray, don't you know me?'

It was James Semple!

The girl was shocked beyond the power of speech. She stood, exactly as she had been standing when he spoke her name, and stared at him. His dress was that of a labourer, except for his coat—an old black overcoat, torn, and indescribably dirty, which had the effect of making him look a thousand times more disreputable than he would have been without it. On his head was a battered felt hat, gray with old age. His face was thin and unshaven, his eyes hungry and wolfish.

'Well! you needn't stare at me like that!' he exclaimed.

But Laura did not hear him. She had burst into tears. She hardly could have told why she wept; for certainly the man deserved his evil fortune. Yet it seemed too horrible that a man whom she had lived with on terms of familiarity should be reduced to this—to actual squalor and hunger.

'You're sorry for me, I see. You've a good heart, Laura. But you won't care to be seen speaking to me,' he added, throwing a furtive glance around him. 'There's a policeman coming up the street. Let's turn down here,' and he led the way into a side-alley. Half reluctantly the girl followed him.

'I say, do you know if there's a warrant out against me?' he whispered, stretching his unsightly face nearer to her.

'No; I think not. I never heard of anything of that kind.'

'Because I've been afraid, you know—horribly afraid. I haven't been able to sleep at night. I couldn't go to prison, Laura. Not for long, you know. It would kill me.'

'Where have you been? And how did you know I was here?'

'I've been in Spain. I worked my passage from Lisbon. And I went to the house in Claremont Gardens one night, after dark, and the old woman who is keeping the place told me where you had gone. I've tramped from London.'

'And how have you lived, all this time?'

'I haven't lived, I've starved. That's what I've done. You never knew what it was to be hungry, I suppose. How would you like to be hungry, not for days, but weeks and weeks—and cold too at the same time, and nowhere to sleep. I couldn't stand it, so I came back and took my chance. I say, Laura, can you lend me any money?'

Laura took out her purse. There were two sovereigns in it, besides some silver. She poured it all into the man's open palm.

'I am not rich now,' she said, with a sad smile; 'I lost nearly all my money.' And she then remembered that it would be two months at least before her purse could be filled again.

'Have you?' said Semple. 'Are you sure you can spare all this?' He picked out one of the sovereigns and held it, as if he intended to return it.

'Oh yes, I can spare it; and you want it so much.'

'Don't I! But you're a good sort, Laura,' returned Semple; slipping the sovereign into his pocket with the rest of the money.

'I'm afraid I must go now,' said the girl,

remembering that it was just possible that they might be observed.

'All right. I'll go back to London. It's easier to pick up coppers there than anywhere else.'

'Why don't you consult a lawyer?' asked Laura suddenly.

'What! Don't you see, I could be caught and put in prison, for the conspiracy, if it were nothing else?'

'Yes; but surely the lawyer might act for you, and get your money for you, even if you lived abroad.'

'I thought of that. But what lawyer would look at me, dressed as I am now? Your two sovereigns will change all that, Laura. I will find a solicitor to take up the case. There ought to be ten thousand pounds for my share of the residue.'

'Far more than that. The Free Church——'

'Yes. What about the Free Church? They get the half-million, don't they?'

'I believe not. Alec gave up his share to them; and they tried to get your share from the executors; but the court decided that they could not prove their case, and had no right to it.'

'Are you sure?' cried Semple, almost mad with excitement.

'I am quite sure. I saw it in the papers about a fortnight ago.'

'You don't say so! What luck!' And with sundry half-articulate cries of wonder and delight, Mr. James Semple disappeared.

Six weeks afterwards he came back to Brighton. It was on a Sunday morning that Laura and he met. She had a headache which had prevented her going to church; and she was enjoying the unwonted repose of the little sitting-room when the door was opened, and Semple walked into the room. He was no longer an outcast dressed in rags. Every article of dress he had on was palpably new;

and except for an irrepressible twitch of the eyelids, he had an air of confidence and display.

'You see I've come back again, Laura,' he said, as soon as the door was closed. 'I didn't forget you. But it was a risk—a tremendous risk. Curtin—that's my solicitor—is careful to impress on me that my getting the money won't save me from prosecution. It's a comfortable truth for him; for he's charged me fifty per cent. for the money he has lent me, —— him, because he knew very well I didn't dare to go to anyone else for it. But how are you?'

'I don't feel very well to-day.'

'I'm sorry for that. Well, I've come a good way to see you. I'm in France, you know—supposed to be in France; and I ran over last night and came down here this morning. I want to pay you the little debt I owe you;' and he counted out the money as he spoke. 'We've made them pay up,' he cried in triumphant tone.

'Indeed,' said Laura.

'Yes. Two hundred and eleven thousand four hundred and nineteen pounds were paid in to my account at the Bank of England on Friday morning. What do you think of that?'

'I'm going to buy a yacht,' he continued, without waiting for an answer. 'One feels more comfortable, safer, in fact, on board ship.'

He ceased talking for a moment, and Laura made no effort to supply the gap.

'I say, Laura,' he exclaimed, 'did you ever hear of such a fool as that fellow Alec—throwing away all that money?'

Laura reddened. It was exactly what she had thought herself; but it was a very different thing to hear it from this man's mouth.

'So I'm the heir after all!' He laughed;

he actually laughed as he spoke. 'And as soon as I've come into my inheritance I've come back to you. I'm not a man to forget old friends or old promises, Laura; and I've come to ask you to let bygones be bygones, and go shares with me in this good luck. You'll marry me, Laura, won't you? And we'll be so jolly! Think of how jolly we will be! Eh, Laura?'

'But I have lost my fortune, Mr. Semple,' she said, without raising her eyes.

'What is that to me?—a flea-bite—a mere flea-bite;' and Mr. Semple drummed on the table pleasantly with the tips of his fingers.

'And you might perhaps find someone who was more attractive, more accomplished, more worthy to be the wife of a rich man than poor me,' said the girl, almost humbly.

'Oh, well; I dare say I might pick almost anywhere now; but we are old friends, and I have always liked you, Laura, so——'

He stretched out his hand and laid it upon hers.

At the touch she sprang to her feet as if she had been stung.

'You wretch!' she cried. 'You cowardly, cruel monster! How dare you ask an honest girl to marry you! Do you think I would have accepted you as you were the other day? As little would I listen to you now!'

He shrank back amazed, angry, insulted—cowering before the girl's scorn.

'You think that because I pitied you and gave you money to save you from starvation that I forgot what a vile being you are. You helped to lay a snare for your cousin, who never so much as lifted a finger against you. You would have seen him sent into penal servitude innocent, that you might get this money. I never heard of such baseness. I could not have conceived that anyone could have been so mean, so cruel!'

'It wasn't my idea; I never knew what was going on.'

'You changed the wills; and you were ready to swear your cousin's liberty away, and let him spend his life in prison, while you—— And you think you can come here and ask me to marry you as if you were not known. What did you take me for? Can you not imagine that a girl would die a thousand times rather than marry such as you? I think you had better go.'

Her last words were not needed. Semple hung his head like a slave caught in a theft, and slunk out of the room.

CHAPTER XXXVIII.

TWO YEARS AFTER.

A TALL bearded man walked slowly up the side of a steep ravine, leading a tired horse by the bridle. His hands were plunged deep in his trousers-pockets, and his brows were knitted in deep thought. He wore the regulation Australian costume—flannel shirt and silk scarf, straw hat, rough trousers, and enormous boots.

It was Alec Lindsay. Two years of the dry bracing air of Australia had done wonders for him. His cheeks and hands were brown as a nut, his muscles strong and springy as when he used to run up the sides of the

Highland hills; not a trace of weakness was left in his frame.

When the ascent was climbed, the traveller came upon a rough path running along the upper edge of the gully, which brought him to a shepherd's hut. This had been Alec's home for the last fifteen months. Here he had lived, contentedly enough, dreaming now and then of the big world so far away, but never hankering after it, deeming it a pleasant piece of excitement if a traveller dropped in with a fortnight-old newspaper in his pocket.

As he drew near the hut, a short, thick-set man with a black beard, which resembled a section of a sweep's brush, appeared at the doorway, and stood waiting for his companion's approach.

'Well?' he inquired, as Alec came up.

'I saw Martin,' said Alec; 'and I ordered the flour, and the other things. The wash for the sheep will be sent over on Saturday.'

Bill Cutbush gave a grunt, by way of acknowledging the information.

'I went round by the post-office.'

'Ah!' growled Bill. 'That's what's made you so late. You didn't get any letters for me, I fancy? No billy-doos, or such-like?'

'There was a letter and a paper for you,' answered Alec, producing them from his pouch.

Bill stared at them as if he were half afraid of them.

'Blest if I ain't forgot how to read such things,' he said, with a short laugh, as he thrust them into his pocket, and turned away.

'I got a letter too,' began Alec. 'I think, Bill——'

Then he saw that his rough-spoken comrade was paying no attention to him, but was striding off to discover what the news was that had travelled so many thousand miles to find him.

So Alec rubbed down Brown Jim, his horse, and fed him. After that he went to the brook and washed himself, and then he walked into the hut. Supper, the never-changing supper of tea, chops, and unleavened bread, was ready cooked; and when that subject had been adequately discussed, Alec lit his pipe and sat down on a log outside the hut to ruminate.

Much had happened during the two years of his exile. His father had died, and Margaret had let the Castle Farm, and the others which the laird had bought back before his death, and had gone to live with Miss Lindsay in Glasgow.

Old Mr. Blake, too, was dead; and Hubert Blake and Sophy had been married for some time. The letter Alec had just received was from Blake; and pulling it out of his pocket he began to read it once more.

'My dear Lindsay' (so ran the letter),

'I see it is of no use to blow you up for not writing—so I spare you. But I have news for you. Your cousin Semple is dead. Poor fellow, I fear his wealth did him little good. You know, I dare say, that he managed to hear of an attorney while he was in Spain, and through this man he succeeded in recovering the quarter of a million to obtain which he did you so grievous a wrong. But he never dared to show his face in England, knowing that if he escaped imprisonment he would have been shunned by everybody.

'I have seen his lawyer, who seems a fairly respectable individual; and he tells me that the two hundred and fifty thousand pounds are intact; and that your cousin left no will. So you and your sister inherit this property.

You must come home at once, and see about it. I believe your sister is to be put into possession of her share very shortly.

'You are a rich man now, Lindsay; and if you choose you may do something towards realizing those schemes of colonization which in your book, "England's Hope," you recommend to all wealthy philanthropists. At least you may as well spend the money in that way; for I feel certain you will get rid of it before long, in one way or another. As for "England's Hope," it has made quite a sensation. It is talked of and quoted everywhere; and really your doctrine that the unskilled labourers who are starving should be helped to emigrate to Australia in large numbers, and settled on virgin land by the two Governments, seems to me the only practical way of solving the difficulty. I quite agree with you in this, that we may expect the agricultural labourers to find less and less work on English farms, so that the distress which comes round as regularly every winter as the first of November, must grow worse every year, unless it is relieved by a remedy which will be in some degree commensurate with the evil.

'But we will talk over all this when we meet. What I want to impress upon you is that you must, as soon as this reaches you, saddle your horse, and make for the nearest seaport. Take the first steamer for England, and as soon as you land come straight to Brighton. We shall be here for four or five months at least. I want to have a long chat with you, and my wife wants to show you the baby, whose faculties (according to his mother) are well-nigh superhuman, and whose beauties and graces are infinite.

'By the way, we lighted upon an old acquaintance of yours the other day, Miss Mowbray. Poor girl, I fancy she has rather a hard life of it. She foolishly invested the greater part of her little fortune in a company which paid high dividends long enough to enable the promoters to sell their shares, and then went to smash. So she lives with some relations as a sort of nursery-governess to a pack of preternaturally ugly children. But I fancy her hard fortune has improved her. My wife has taken a great fancy to her, chiefly, I believe, on account of her courage in giving evidence on a certain occasion, and on account of her refusing James Semple, when he wanted to marry her last year.

'Now, good-bye, and remember to come to Brighton the moment your ship comes in.

'Yours always,

'HUBERT BLAKE.'

By the time Alec's pipe was finished, Bill Cutbush had returned to the hut. He was very quiet and subdued in his manner. Evidently the contents of his letter had touched him deeply; but he said not a word about it.

'Bill,' said Alec, before they separated for the night, 'I have had an important letter from England: and I am going home. I spoke to Martin; and he will send someone to take my place to-morrow.'

'When d'you start?' asked Bill, after a pause.

'At daybreak.'

'What are you going to do with Brown Jim?'

'I shall ride him to Clifford's, and catch the stage there.'

'You think of selling him?'

'I shall leave him to you, Bill.'

'For my own?'

'Of course.'

'Thank'ee.'

'Good-night, Bill.'

Half an hour afterwards Alec suddenly awoke.

'Who's there?' he shouted.

'It's only me,' said the voice of Bill Cutbush. 'I say, y'know, it was sort of partickler good in you to give me Brown Jim. He's the best hoss for a long way round. I'll take good care on him. Thought you'd like to know.'

And before Alec had time to reply, Bill had vanished.

*   *   *   *   *

Before two months had passed, Alec was once more in London. And without waiting to see the solicitor who had charge of his late cousin's property, he went down to Brighton the same day.

To his disappointment, however, he found that Blake and his wife were not at home, and would not probably be back till the evening. Alec spent the rest of the day in wandering about the pier and the streets, feeling more lonely than he had been in the Australian bush.

It was late in the afternoon, and he was strolling aimlessly along the seashore, when happening to look towards the cliffs he caught sight of Laura Mowbray.

Yes, it was she; a glad surprise shining in her eyes. Alec rushed up to her, holding out both his hands.

'Oh, how are you? I am so glad to see you!' he cried.

Laura gave him her right hand without speaking, but Alec seized her left as well, and held it, while his eyes devoured her face.

'Won't you give me a word of welcome?' he asked.

'Welcome back to England!' she said, gently disengaging her hands.

Then they walked on side by side.

'When did you return?' asked Laura.

'I only reached London this morning.'

'Had you a pleasant voyage?'

'Yes; but I want to hear about you. I want to know so much.'

'No, no; you shall tell me all about Australia, and what you have been doing all this time.'

There were plenty of topics for conversation, and an hour went by before they noticed that the sun was near his setting.

'I must take the children home,' said Laura. 'They are under my charge, you know.'

'The children? Where are they?'

'Playing over there. Oh! I have been keeping an eye on them all the time. I have not been so careless as you think.'

'You cannot imagine,' said Alec, as they walked over to the children's encampment, 'how strange it seems to me that I am here, walking by your side. I can hardly believe it to be true.'

Laura smiled, but she said nothing by way of reply; and just then two pert-looking little girls came running up and claimed her attention. Alec drew back a little, and watched the group. He could not help seeing that in some subtle way Laura was greatly changed. Her manner was gentle and self-forgetful. The very tones of her voice had altered.

Presently the children scampered off again, and Alec rejoined his companion.

'Do you know what I was thinking of just now?' he said.

Something in his voice startled her. He did not wait for an answer, but went on:

'I was thinking of an afternoon in the garden at Glendhu, half a dozen years ago.'

'Some things are best forgotten,' she murmured, hardly knowing what she said.

'I was only a foolish boy then,' went on

Alec, 'but I think my heart has never changed.'

'Please stop, Mr. Lindsay. Indeed I cannot listen to you.'

'Laura—you are not—engaged?'

'No; oh no!'

'Then why won't you listen? You did not doubt me then. Why should you doubt me now?'

'I don't doubt you. But it can never, never be.'

'You think I am hasty. It may seem so, but I have been longing to tell you this for weeks and months. And you know my heart was always yours.'

'Oh, Mr. Lindsay, I entreat you not to say any more! I should not have allowed you to go on.'

'Why? If I can win your love, Laura——'

'No, no; you do not really know me. You do not understand.'

'I only understand one thing—I love you. Laura, you won't refuse me?'

'But I have been so heartless, so unprincipled, so selfish, so——' the rest was lost in tears.

'Hush, hush! I won't have you say such things.'

'But they are true.'

'Laura, just one word,' whispered Alec, gently taking her hand in his. 'Can you care for me? Look at me, dearest.'

'It is better not,' she said, trying to withdraw her hand. 'See, there are Mr. and Mrs. Blake coming down the cliff.'

'They don't see us yet. There is time for you to hear me and make me happy.'

'Would it make you happy? Are you sure?' asked Laura; and the sunlight seemed to play for a moment on her face.

'Can you doubt it? Come; let us forget the last three years, and imagine that we are boy and girl again at Glendhu. Will you? And let me whisper, "Can you love me, Laura?"'

'Oh, Alec, in my heart I loved you even then!'

THE END.

[December, 1887.

A LIST OF BOOKS
PUBLISHED BY
CHATTO & WINDUS,
214, PICCADILLY, LONDON, W.

Sold by all Booksellers, or sent post-free for the published price by the Publishers:

About.—The Fellah: An Egyptian Novel. By EDMOND ABOUT. Translated by Sir RANDAL ROBERTS. Post 8vo, illustrated boards, 2s.; cloth limp, 2s. 6d.

Adams (W. Davenport), Works by:
A Dictionary of the Drama. Being a comprehensive Guide to the Plays, Playwrights, Players, and Playhouses of the United Kingdom and America, from the Earliest to the Present Times. Crown 8vo, half-bound, 12s. 6d. [*Preparing.*
Quips and Quiddities. Selected by W. DAVENPORT ADAMS. Post 8vo, cloth limp, 2s. 6d.

Advertising, A History of, from the Earliest Times. Illustrated by Anecdotes, Curious Specimens, and Notices of Successful Advertisers. By HENRY SAMPSON. Crown 8vo, with Coloured Frontispiece and Illustrations, cloth gilt, 7s. 6d.

Agony Column (The) of "The Times," from 1800 to 1870. Edited, with an Introduction, by ALICE CLAY. Post 8vo, cloth limp, 2s. 6d.

Aidé (Hamilton), Works by:
Post 8vo, illustrated boards, 2s. each.
Carr of Carrlyon. | Confidences.

Alexander (Mrs.), Novels by:
Post 8vo, illustrated boards, 2s. each.
Maid, Wife, or Widow?
Valerie's Fate.

Allen (Grant), Works by:
Crown 8vo, cloth extra, 6s. each.
The Evolutionist at Large. Second Edition, revised.
Vignettes from Nature.
Colin Clout's Calendar.

ALLEN (GRANT), *continued*—
Strange Stories. With Frontispiece by GEORGE DU MAURIER. Cr. 8vo, cl. ex., 6s.; post 8vo, illust. bds., 2s.
Philistia: A Novel. Crown 8vo, cloth extra, 3s. 6d.; post 8vo, illust. bds., 2s.
Babylon: A Novel. Post 8vo, illust. boards, 2s.
For Maimie's Sake: A Tale of Love and Dynamite. Cr. 8vo, cl. ex., 6s.
In all Shades: A Novel. New and Cheaper Edition. Crown 8vo, cloth extra, 3s. 6d.
The Beckoning Hand, &c. With a Frontispiece by TOWNLEY GREEN. Crown 8vo, cloth extra, 6s.

Architectural Styles, A Handbook of. Translated from the German of A. ROSENGARTEN, by W. COLLETT-SANDARS. Crown 8vo, cloth extra, with 639 Illustrations, 7s. 6d.

Arnold.—Bird Life in England. By EDWIN LESTER ARNOLD. Crown 8vo, cloth extra, 6s.

Artemus Ward:
Artemus Ward's Works: The Works of CHARLES FARRER BROWNE, better known as ARTEMUS WARD. With Portrait and Facsimile. Crown 8vo, cloth extra, 7s. 6d.
The Genial Showman: Life and Adventures of Artemus Ward. By EDWARD P. HINGSTON. With a Frontispiece. Cr. 8vo, cl. extra, 3s. 6d.

Art (The) of Amusing: A Collection of Graceful Arts, Games, Tricks, Puzzles, and Charades. By FRANK BELLEW. With 300 Illustrations. Cr. 8vo, cloth extra, 4s. 6d.

Ashton (John), Works by:
Crown 8vo, cloth extra, 7s. 6d. each.
A History of the Chap-Books of the Eighteenth Century. With nearly 400 Illustrations, engraved in facsimile of the originals.
Social Life in the Reign of Queen Anne. From Original Sources. With nearly 100 Illustrations.
Humour, Wit, and Satire of the Seventeenth Century. With nearly 100 Illustrations.
English Caricature and Satire on Napoleon the First. With 120 Illustrations. [Preparing.

Bacteria.—A Synopsis of the Bacteria and Yeast Fungi and Allied Species. By W. B. GROVE, B.A. With 67 Illusts. Crown 8vo, cl. extra, 3s. 6d.

Bankers, A Handbook of London; together with Lists of Bankers from 1677. By F. G. HILTON PRICE. Crown 8vo, cloth extra, 7s 6d

Bardsley (Rev. C.W.), Works by:
Crown 8vo, cloth extra, 7s. 6d. each.
English Surnames: Their Sources and Significations. Third Ed., revised.
Curiosities of Puritan Nomenclature.

Bartholomew Fair, Memoirs of. By HENRY MORLEY. With 100 Illusts. Crown 8vo, cloth extra, 7s. 6d.

Beaconsfield, Lord: A Biography. By T. P. O'CONNOR, M.P. Sixth Edition, with a New Preface. Crown 8vo, cloth extra, 7s. 6d.

Beauchamp. — Grantley Grange: A Novel. By SHELSLEY BEAUCHAMP. Post 8vo, illust. bds., 2s.

Beautiful Pictures by British Artists: A Gathering of Favourites from our Picture Galleries. All engraved on Steel in the highest style of Art. Edited, with Notices of the Artists, by SYDNEY ARMYTAGE, M.A Imperial 4to, cloth extra gilt and gilt edges 21s.

Bechstein. — As Pretty as Seven, and other German Stories. Collected by LUDWIG BECHSTEIN. With Additional Tales by the Brothers GRIMM, and 100 Illusts. by RICHTER. Small 4to, green and gold, 6s. 6d. gilt edges, 7s. 6d.

Beerbohm. — Wanderings in Patagonia; or, Life among the Ostrich Hunters. By JULIUS BEERBOHM. With Illusts. Crown 8vo, cloth extra, 3s. 6d.

Belgravia. One Shilling Monthly.
A New Serial Story by W. CLARK RUSSELL, entitled The Frozen Pirate, began in the JULY Number.—Two New Serial Stories will begin in the Number for JANUARY, 1888, and will be continued through the year: Undercurrents, by the Author of "Phyllis;" and The Blackhall Ghosts, by SARAH TYTLER.
₂ Now ready, the Volume for JULY to OCTOBER, 1887, cloth extra, gilt edges, 7s. 6d.; Cases for binding Vols., 2s. each.

Belgravia Holiday Number, 1887. Demy 8vo. with Illustrations, 1s.

Belgravia Annual, 1887: A Collection of Powerful Short Stories, each complete in itself. With Illustrations. Demy 8vo, 1s. [Nov. 10.

Bennett (W.C., LL.D.), Works by:
Post 8vo, cloth limp, 2s. each.
A Ballad History of England.
Songs for Sailors.

Besant (Walter) and James Rice, Novels by. Crown 8vo, cloth extra, 3s. 6d. each; post 8vo, illust. boards, 2s. each; cloth limp, 2s. 6d. each.
Ready-Money Mortiboy.
With Harp and Crown.
This Son of Vulcan.
My Little Girl
The Case of Mr. Lucraft.
The Golden Butterfly.
By Celia's Arbour.
The Monks of Thelema.
'Twas in Trafalgar's Bay.
The Seamy Side.
The Ten Years' Tenant.
The Chaplain of the Fleet.

Besant (Walter), Novels by:
Crown 8vo, cloth extra, 3s. 6d. each; post 8vo, illust. boards, 2s. each; cloth limp, 2s. 6d. each.
All Sorts and Conditions of Men: An Impossible Story. With Illustrations by FRED. BARNARD.
The Captains' Room, &c. With Frontispiece by E. J. WHEELER.
All in a Garden Fair. With 6 Illusts. by H. FURNISS.
Dorothy Forster. With Frontispiece by CHARLES GREEN.
Uncle Jack, and other Stories.

Besant (Walter), *continued—*
Crown 8vo, cloth extra, 3s. 6d. each.
Children of Gibeon.
The World Went Very Well Then.
With Illustrations by A. Forestier.

The Art of Fiction. Demy 8vo, 1s.
Fifty Years Ago; or, The Queen's Accession. With nearly 150 full-page Plates and Woodcuts. Demy 8vo, cloth extra, 16s. [*Preparing.*
The Eulogy of Richard Jefferies: A Memoir. Demy 8vo, cloth extra, 9s. [*Preparing.*

Library Edition of the Novels of
Besant and Rice.
Now issuing, a choicely-printed Library Edition of the Novels of Messrs. Besant *and* Rice. *The Volumes are printed from new type on a large crown 8vo page, and handsomely bound in cloth. Price Six Shillings each. The First Volumes are*—
Ready-Money Mortiboy. With Portrait of James Rice, etched by Daniel A. Wehrschmidt, and a New Preface by Walter Besant.
My Little Girl.
With Harp and Crown.
This Son of Vulcan.
The Golden Butterfly. With Etched Portrait of Walter Besant. [*Nov.*
The Monks of Thelema.
By Celia's Arbour.
The Chaplain of the Fleet.
The Seamy Side. &c. &c.

Betham-Edwards (M.), Novels by:
Felicia. Cr. 8vo, cloth extra, 3s. 6d.; post 8vo, illust. bds., 2s.
Kitty. Post 8vo, illust. bds., 2s.

Bewick (Thos.) and his Pupils.
By Austin Dobson. With 95 Illustrations. Square 8vo, cloth extra, 10s. 6d.

Birthday Books:—
The Starry Heavens: A Poetical Birthday Book. Square 8vo, handsomely bound in cloth, 2s. 6d.
The Lowell Birthday Book. With Illusts. Small 8vo, cloth extra, 4s. 6d.

Blackburn's (Henry) Art Handbooks. Demy 8vo, Illustrated, uniform in size for binding.
Academy Notes, separate years, from 1875 to 1886, each 1s.
Academy Notes, 1887. With numerous Illustrations. 1s.
Academy Notes, 1875-79. Complete in One Vol., with nearly 600 Illusts. in Facsimile. Demy 8vo, cloth limp, 6s.

Blackburn (Henry), *continued—*
Academy Notes, 1880-84. Complete in One Volume, with about 700 Facsimile Illustrations. Cloth limp, 6s.
Grosvenor Notes, 1877. 6d.
Grosvenor Notes, separate years, from 1878 to 1886, each 1s.
Grosvenor Notes, 1887. With numerous Illusts. 1s.
Grosvenor Notes, Vol. I., 1877-82. With upwards of 300 Illustrations. Demy 8vo, cloth limp, 6s.
Grosvenor Notes, Vol. II., 1883-87. With upwards of 300 Illustrations. Demy 8vo, cloth limp, 6s.
The English Pictures at the National Gallery. 114 Illustrations. 1s.
The Old Masters at the National Gallery. 128 Illustrations. 1s. 6d.
A Complete Illustrated Catalogue to the National Gallery. With Notes by H. Blackburn, and 242 Illusts. Demy 8vo, cloth limp, 3s.

The Paris Salon, 1887. With about 300 Facsimile Sketches. Demy 8vo, 3s.

Blake (William): Etchings from his Works. By W. B. Scott. With descriptive Text. Folio, half-bound boards, India Proofs, 21s.

Boccaccio's Decameron; or, Ten Days' Entertainment. Translated into English, with an Introduction by Thomas Wright, F.S.A. With Portrait and Stothard's beautiful Copperplates. Cr. 8vo, cloth extra, gilt, 7s. 6d.

Bourne (H. R. Fox), Works by:
English Merchants: Memoirs in Illustration of the Progress of British Commerce. With numerous Illustrations. Cr. 8vo, cloth extra, 7s. 6d.
English Newspapers: Contributions to the History of Journalism. Two vols., demy 8vo, cloth extra, 25s.

Bowers'(G.) Hunting Sketches:
Oblong 4to, half-bound boards, 21s. each.
Canters in Crampshire.
Leaves from a Hunting Journal. Coloured in facsimile of the originals.

Boyle (Frederick), Works by:
Crown 8vo, cloth extra, 3s. 6d. each; post 8vo, illustrated boards, 2s. each.
Camp Notes: Stories of Sport and Adventure in Asia, Africa, and America.
Savage Life: Adventures of a Globe Trotter.

Chronicles of No-Man's Land. Post 8vo, illust. boards, 2s.

BOOKS PUBLISHED BY

Brand's Observations on Popular Antiquities, chiefly Illustrating the Origin of our Vulgar Customs, Ceremonies, and Superstitions. With the Additions of Sir HENRY ELLIS. Crown 8vo, with Illustrations, 7s. 6d.

Bret Harte, Works by:

Bret Harte's Collected Works. Arranged and Revised by the Author. Complete in Five Vols., crown 8vo, cloth extra, 6s. each.
  Vol. I. COMPLETE POETICAL AND DRAMATIC WORKS. With Steel Portrait, and Introduction by Author.
  Vol. II. EARLIER PAPERS—LUCK OF ROARING CAMP, and other Sketches—BOHEMIAN PAPERS — SPANISH AND AMERICAN LEGENDS.
  Vol. III. TALES OF THE ARGONAUTS—EASTERN SKETCHES.
  Vol. IV. GABRIEL CONROY.
  Vol. V. STORIES — CONDENSED NOVELS, &c.

The Select Works of Bret Harte, in Prose and Poetry. With Introductory Essay by J. M. BELLEW, Portrait of the Author, and 50 Illustrations. Crown 8vo cloth extra, 7s. 6d.

Bret Harte's Complete Poetical Works. Author's Copyright Edition. Beautifully printed on hand-made paper and bound in buckram. Cr. 8vo, 4s. 6d.

Gabriel Conroy: A Novel. Post 8vo, illustrated boards, 2s.

An Heiress of Red Dog, and other Stories. Post 8vo, illust. boards, 2s.

The Twins of Table Mountain. Fcap. 8vo, picture cover, 1s.

Luck of Roaring Camp, and other Sketches. Post 8vo, illust. bds., 2s.

Jeff Briggs's Love Story. Fcap. 8vo, picture cover, 1s. [2s. 6d.

Flip. Post 8vo, illust. bds., 2s.; cl. limp,

Californian Stories (including THE TWINS OF TABLE MOUNTAIN, JEFF BRIGGS'S LOVE STORY, &c.) Post 8vo, illustrated boards, 2s.

Maruja: A Novel. Post 8vo, illust. boards, 2s.; cloth limp, 2s. 6d.

The Queen of the Pirate Isle. With 28 original Drawings by KATE GREENAWAY, Reproduced in Colours by EDMUND EVANS. Sm. 4to, bds., 5s.

A Phyllis of the Sierras, &c. Post 8vo, illustrated bds, 2s.; cl., 2s. 6d.

Brewer (Rev. Dr.), Works by:

The Reader's Handbook of Allusions, References, Plots, and Stories. Twelfth Thousand. With Appendix, containing a COMPLETE ENGLISH BIBLIOGRAPHY. Cr. 8vo, cloth 7s. 6d.

Authors and their Works, with the Dates: Being the Appendices to "The Reader's Handbook," separately printed. Cr. 8vo, cloth limp, 2s.

BREWER (REV. DR.), *continued*—
A Dictionary of Miracles: Imitative, Realistic, and Dogmatic. Crown 8vo, cloth extra, 7s. 6d.; half-bound, 9s.

Brewster (Sir David), Works by:

More Worlds than One: The Creed of the Philosopher and the Hope of the Christian. With Plates. Post 8vo, cloth extra, 4s. 6d.

The Martyrs of Science: Lives of GALILEO, TYCHO BRAHE, and KEPLER. With Portraits. Post 8vo, cloth extra, 4s. 6d.

Letters on Natural Magic. A New Edition, with numerous Illustrations, and Chapters on the Being and Faculties of Man, and Additional Phenomena of Natural Magic, by J. A. SMITH. Post 8vo, cl. ex., 4s. 6d.

Brillat-Savarin.—Gastronomy as a Fine Art. By BRILLAT-SAVARIN. Translated by R. E. ANDERSON, M.A. Post 8vo, cloth limp, 2s. 6d.

Buchanan's (Robert) Works:

Crown 8vo, cloth extra, 6s. each.
Ballads of Life, Love, and Humour. Frontispiece by ARTHUR HUGHES.
Undertones. | **London Poems.**
The Book of Orm.
White Rose and Red: A Love Story.
Idylls and Legends of Inverburn.
Selected Poems of Robert Buchanan With a Frontispiece by T. DALZIEL.
The Hebrid Isles: Wanderings in the Land of Lorne and the Outer Hebrides. With Frontispiece by WILLIAM SMALL.
A Poet's Sketch-Book: Selections from the Prose Writings of ROBERT BUCHANAN.
The Earthquake; or, Six Days and a Sabbath.
The City of Dream: An Epic Poem.
Robert Buchanan's Complete Poetical Works. With Steel-plate Portrait. Crown 8vo, cloth extra, 7s. 6d.

Crown 8vo, cloth extra, 3s. 6d. each post 8vo, illust. boards, 2s. each.
The Shadow of the Sword.
A Child of Nature. With a Frontispiece.
God and the Man. With Illustrations by FRED. BARNARD.
The Martyrdom of Madeline. With Frontispiece by A. W. COOPER.
Love Me for Ever. With a Frontispiece by P. MACNAB.
Annan Water. | **The New Abelard.**
Foxglove Manor.
Matt: A Story of a Caravan.
The Master of the Mine.

The Heir of Linne: A Romance. Two Vols., crown 8vo.

Bunyan's Pilgrim's Progress.
Edited by Rev. T. SCOTT. With 17 Steel Plates by STOTHARD engraved by GOODALL, and numerous Woodcuts. Crown 8vo, cloth extra, gilt, 7s. 6d.

Burnett (Mrs.), Novels by:
Surly Tim, and other Stories. Post 8vo, illustrated boards, 2s.

Fcap. 8vo, picture cover, 1s. each.
Kathleen Mavourneen.
Lindsay's Luck.
Pretty Polly Pemberton.

Burton (Captain).—The Book of the Sword: Being a History of the Sword and its Use in all Countries, from the Earliest Times. By RICHARD F. BURTON. With over 400 Illustrations. Square 8vo, cloth extra, 32s.

Burton (Robert):
The Anatomy of Melancholy. A New Edition, complete, corrected and enriched by Translations of the Classical Extracts. Demy 8vo, cloth extra, 7s. 6d.

Melancholy Anatomised: Being an Abridgment, for popular use, of BURTON'S ANATOMY OF MELANCHOLY. Post 8vo, cloth limp, 2s. 6d.

Byron (Lord):
Byron's Letters and Journals. With Notices of his Life. By THOMAS MOORE. A Reprint of the Original Edition. Cr. 8vo, cloth extra, 7s. 6d.

Byron's Don Juan. Complete in One Vol., post 8vo, cloth limp, 2s.

Caine (T. Hall), Novels by:
The Shadow of a Crime. Cr. 8vo, cloth extra, 3s. 6d.; post 8vo, illustrated boards, 2s.

A Son of Hagar. New and Cheaper Edition. Crown 8vo, cloth extra, 3s. 6d.

The Deemster: A Romance of the Isle of Man. Three Vols., cr. 8vo.

Cameron (Comdr.).— The Cruise of the "Black Prince" Privateer, Commanded by ROBERT HAWKINS, Master Mariner. By Commander V. LOVETT CAMERON, R.N., C.B., D.C.L. With Frontispiece and Vignette by P. MACNAB. Crown 8vo, cl. ex., 5s.

Cameron (Mrs. H. Lovett),
Novels by:
Crown 8vo, cloth extra, 3s. 6d. each post 8vo, illustrated boards, 2s. each.
Juliet's Guardian. | Deceivers Ever.

Carlyle (Thomas):
On the Choice of Books. By THOMAS CARLYLE. With a Life of the Author by R. H. SHEPHERD. New and Revised Edition, post 8vo, cloth extra, Illustrated, 1s. 6d.

The Correspondence of Thomas Carlyle and Ralph Waldo Emerson 1834 to 1872. Edited by CHARLES ELIOT NORTON. With Portraits. Two Vols., crown 8vo, cloth extra, 24s.

Chapman's (George) Works:
Vol. I. contains the Plays complete, including the doubtful ones. Vol. II., the Poems and Minor Translations, with an Introductory Essay by ALGERNON CHARLES SWINBURNE. Vol. III., the Translations of the Iliad and Odyssey. Three Vols., crown 8vo, cloth extra, 18s.; or separately, 6s. each.

Chatto & Jackson.—A Treatise on Wood Engraving, Historical and Practical. By WM. ANDREW CHATTO and JOHN JACKSON. With an Additional Chapter by HENRY G. BOHN; and 450 fine Illustrations. A Reprint of the last Revised Edition. Large 4to, half-bound, 28s.

Chaucer:
Chaucer for Children: A Golden Key. By Mrs. H.R. HAWEIS. With Eight Coloured Pictures and numerous Woodcuts by the Author. New Ed., small 4to, cloth extra, 6s.
Chaucer for Schools. By Mrs. H. R. HAWEIS. Demy 8vo. cloth limp, 2s.6d.

Chronicle (The) of the Coach:
Charing Cross to Ilfracombe. By J.D CHAMPLIN. With 75 Illustrations by EDWARD L. CHICHESTER. Square 8vo, cloth extra, 7s. 6d.

Clodd.— Myths and Dreams.
By EDWARD CLODD, F.R.A.S., Author of "The Childhood of Religions," &c. Crown 8vo, cloth extra, 5s.

Cobban.—The Cure of Souls:
A Story. By J. MACLAREN COBBAN. Post 8vo, illustrated boards, 2s.

Coleman.—Curly: An Actor's Story. By JOHN COLEMAN. Illustrated by J. C. DOLLMAN. Crown 8vo, 1s.; cloth, 1s. 6d.

Colquhoun.—Every Inch a Soldier: A Novel. By M. J. COLQUHOUN. Three Vols., crown 8vo.

Collins (Wilkie), Novels by:
Crown 8vo, cloth extra, Illustrated, 3s. 6d. each; post 8vo, illustrated bds., 2s. each; cloth limp, 2s. 6d. each.
Antonina. Illust. by Sir JOHN GILBERT.
Basil. Illustrated by Sir JOHN GILBERT and J. MAHONEY.
Hide and Seek. Illustrated by Sir JOHN GILBERT and J. MAHONEY.
The Dead Secret. Illustrated by Sir JOHN GILBERT.
Queen of Hearts. Illustrated by Sir JOHN GILBERT.
My Miscellanies. With a Steel-plate Portrait of WILKIE COLLINS.
The Woman in White. With Illustrations by Sir JOHN GILBERT and F. A. FRASER.
The Moonstone. With Illustrations by G. DU MAURIER and F. A. FRASER.
Man and Wife. Illust. by W. SMALL.
Poor Miss Finch. Illustrated by G. DU MAURIER and EDWARD HUGHES.
Miss or Mrs.? With Illustrations by S. L. FILDES and HENRY WOODS.
The New Magdalen. Illustrated by G. DU MAURIER and C. S. REINHARDT.
The Frozen Deep. Illustrated by G. DU MAURIER and J. MAHONEY.
The Law and the Lady. Illustrated by S. L. FILDES and SYDNEY HALL.
The Two Destinies.
The Haunted Hotel. Illustrated by ARTHUR HOPKINS.
The Fallen Leaves.
Jezebel's Daughter.
The Black Robe.
Heart and Science: A Story of the Present Time.
"I Say No."
The Evil Genius.

Little Novels. Cr. 8vo, cl. ex., 3s. 6d.

Collins (Mortimer), Novels by:
Crown 8vo, cloth extra, 3s. 6d. each; post 8vo, illustrated boards, 2s. each.
Sweet Anne Page. | Transmigration.
From Midnight to Midnight.

A Fight with Fortune. Post 8vo, illustrated boards, 2s.

Collins (Mortimer & Frances), Novels by:
Crown 8vo, cloth extra, 3s. 6d. each; post 8vo, illustrated boards, 2s. each.
Blacksmith and Scholar.
The Village Comedy.
You Play Me False.

Post 8vo, illustrated boards, 2s. each.
Sweet and Twenty. | Frances.

Collins (C. Allston).—The Bar Sinister: A Story. By C. ALLSTON COLLINS. Post 8vo, illustrated bds., 2s.

Colman's Humorous Works: "Broad Grins," "My Nightgown and Slippers," and other Humorous Works, Prose and Poetical, of GEORGE COLMAN. With Life by G. B. BUCKSTONE, and Frontispiece by HOGARTH. Crown 8vo cloth extra, gilt, 7s. 6d.

Convalescent Cookery: A Family Handbook. By CATHERINE RYAN. Crown 8vo, 1s.; cloth, 1s. 6d.

Conway (Moncure D.), Works by:
Demonology and Devil-Lore. Two Vols., royal 8vo. with 65 Illusts., 28s.
A Necklace of Stories. Illustrated by W. J. HENNESSY. Square 8vo, cloth extra, 6s.
Pine and Palm: A Novel. Two Vols., crown 8vo.

Cook (Dutton), Works by:
Crown 8vo, cloth extra, 6s. each.
Hours with the Players. With a Steel Plate Frontispiece.
Nights at the Play: A View of the English Stage.

Leo: A Novel. Post 8vo, illustrated boards, 2s.
Paul Foster's Daughter. crown 8vo, cloth extra, 3s. 6d.; post 8vo, illustrated boards, 2s.

Copyright.—A Handbook of English and Foreign Copyright in Literary and Dramatic Works. By SIDNEY JERROLD, of the Middle Temple, Esq., Barrister-at-Law. Post 8vo, cloth limp, 2s. 6d.

Cornwall.—Popular Romances of the West of England; or, The Drolls, Traditions, and Superstitions of Old Cornwall. Collected and Edited by ROBERT HUNT, F.R.S. New and Revised Edition, with Additions, and Two Steel-plate Illustrations by GEORGE CRUIKSHANK. Crown 8vo, cloth extra, 7s. 6d.

Craddock.—The Prophet of the Great Smoky Mountains. By CHARLES EGBERT CRADDOCK Post 8vo, illus. bds., 2s cloth limp, 2s. 6d.

Creasy.—Memoirs of Eminent Etonians: with Notices of the Early History of Eton College. By Sir EDWARD CREASY, Author of "The Fifteen Decisive Battles of the World." Crown 8vo, cloth extra, gilt, with 13 Portraits, 7s. 6d.

CHATTO & WINDUS, PICCADILLY. 7

Cruikshank (George):
The Comic Almanack. Complete in Two Series: The First from 1835 to 1843; the Second from 1844 to 1853. A Gathering of the Best Humour of Thackeray, Hood, Mayhew, Albert Smith, A'Beckett, Robert Brough, &c. With 2,000 Woodcuts and Steel Engravings by Cruikshank, Hine, Landells, &c. Crown 8vo, cloth gilt, two very thick volumes, 7s. 6d. each.

The Life of George Cruikshank. By Blanchard Jerrold, Author of "The Life of Napoleon III.," &c. With 84 Illustrations. New and Cheaper Edition, enlarged, with Additional Plates, and a very carefully compiled Bibliography. Crown 8vo, cloth extra, 7s. 6d.

Robinson Crusoe. A beautiful reproduction of Major's Edition, with 37 Woodcuts and Two Steel Plates by George Cruikshank, choicely printed. Crown 8vo, cloth extra, 7s. 6d.

Cumming (C. F. Gordon), Works by:
Demy 8vo, cloth extra, 8s. 6d. each.
In the Hebrides. With Autotype Facsimile and numerous full-page Illustrations.
In the Himalayas and on the Indian Plains. With numerous Illustrations.
Via Cornwall to Egypt. With a Photogravure Frontispiece. Demy 8vo, cloth extra, 7s. 6d.

Cussans.—Handbook of Heraldry; with Instructions for Tracing Pedigrees and Deciphering Ancient MSS., &c. By John E. Cussans. Entirely New and Revised Edition, illustrated with over 400 Woodcuts and Coloured Plates. Crown 8vo, cloth extra, 7s. 6d.

Cyples.—Hearts of Gold: A Novel. By William Cyples. Crown 8vo, cloth extra, 3s. 6d.; post 8vo, illustrated boards, 2s.

Daniel.—Merrie England in the Olden Time. By George Daniel. With Illustrations by Robt. Cruikshank. Crown 8vo, cloth extra, 3s. 6d.

Daudet.—The Evangelist; or, Port Salvation. By Alphonse Daudet. Translated by C. Harry Meltzer. With Portrait of the Author. Crown 8vo, cloth extra, 3s. 6d.; post 8vo, illust. boards, 2s.

Davies (Dr. N. E.), Works by:
Crown 8vo, 1s. each; cloth limp, 1s. 6d. each.
One Thousand Medical Maxims.
Nursery Hints: A Mother's Guide.
Aids to Long Life. Crown 8vo, 2s.; cloth limp, 2s. 6d.

Davies' (Sir John) Complete Poetical Works, including Psalms I. to L. in Verse, and other hitherto Unpublished MSS., for the first time Collected and Edited, with Memorial-Introduction and Notes, by the Rev. A. B. Grosart, D.D. Two Vols., crown 8vo, cloth boards, 12s.

De Maistre.—A Journey Round My Room. By Xavier de Maistre. Translated by Henry Attwell. Post 8vo, cloth limp, 2s. 6d.

De Mille.—A Castle in Spain: A Novel. By James De Mille. With a Frontispiece. Crown 8vo, cloth extra, 3s. 6d.; post 8vo, illust. bds., 2s.

Derwent (Leith), Novels by:
Crown 8vo, cloth extra, 3s. 6d. each; post 8vo, illustrated boards, 2s. each.
Our Lady of Tears. | Circe's Lovers.

Dickens (Charles), Novels by:
Post 8vo, illustrated boards, 2s. each.
Sketches by Boz. | Nicholas Nickleby.
Pickwick Papers. | Oliver Twist.

The Speeches of Charles Dickens, 1841–1870. With a New Bibliography, revised and enlarged. Edited and Prefaced by Richard Herne Shepherd. Cr. 8vo, cloth extra, 6s.—Also a Smaller Edition, in the *Mayfair Library*. Post 8vo, cloth limp, 2s. 6d.

About England with Dickens. By Alfred Rimmer. With 57 Illustrations by C. A. Vanderhoof, Alfred Rimmer, and others. Sq. 8vo, cloth extra, 10s. 6d.

Dictionaries:
A Dictionary of Miracles: Imitative, Realistic, and Dogmatic. By the Rev. E. C. Brewer, LL.D. Crown 8vo, cloth extra, 7s. 6d.; hf.-bound, 9s.

The Reader's Handbook of Allusions, References, Plots, and Stories. By the Rev. E. C. Brewer, LL.D. With an Appendix, containing a Complete English Bibliography. Eleventh Thousand. Crown 8vo, 1,400 pages, cloth extra, 7s. 6d.

Authors and their Works, with the Dates. Being the Appendices to "The Reader's Handbook," separately printed. By the Rev. Dr. Brewer. Crown 8vo, cloth limp, 2s

BOOKS PUBLISHED BY

DICTIONARIES, *continued*—
Familiar Short Sayings of Great Men. With Historical and Explanatory Notes. By SAMUEL A. BENT, M.A. Fifth Edition, revised and enlarged. Cr. 8vo, cloth extra, 7s 6d.
A Dictionary of the Drama: Being a comprehensive Guide to the Plays, Playwrights, Players, and Playhouses of the United Kingdom and America, from the Earliest to the Present Times. By W DAVENPORT ADAMS. A thick volume, crown 8vo, half-bound, 12s. 6d. [*In preparation*.
The Slang Dictionary: Etymological, Historical, and Anecdotal. Crown 8vo, cloth extra, 6s. 6d.
Women of the Day: A Biographical Dictionary. By FRANCES HAYS. Cr. 8vo, cloth extra, 5s.
Words, Facts, and Phrases: A Dictionary of Curious, Quaint, and Out-of-the-Way Matters. By ELIEZER EDWARDS. New and Cheaper Issue. Cr. 8vo, cl. ex., 7s. 6d. ; hf.-bd., 9s.

Diderot.—The Paradox of Acting. Translated, with Annotations, from Diderot's "Le Paradoxe sur le Comédien," by WALTER HERRIES POLLOCK. With a Preface by HENRY IRVING. Cr. 8vo, in parchment, 4s. 6d.

Dobson (W. T.), Works by:
Post 8vo, cloth limp, 2s. 6d. each.
Literary Frivolities, Fancies, Follies, and Frolics. [cities.
Poetical Ingenuities and Eccentri-

Doran. — Memories of our Great Towns; with Anecdotic Gleanings concerning their Worthies and their Oddities. By Dr. JOHN DORAN, F.S.A. With 38 Illusts. New and Cheaper Edit. Cr. 8vo, cl. extra, 7s. 6d.

Drama, A Dictionary of the. Being a comprehensive Guide to the Plays, Playwrights, Players, and Playhouses of the United Kingdom and America, from the Earliest to the Present Times. By W. DAVENPORT ADAMS. (Uniform with BREWER'S "Reader's Handbook.") Crown 8vo, half-bound, 12s. 6d. [*In preparation*.

Dramatists, The Old. Cr. 8vo, cl. ex., Vignette Portraits, 6s. per Vol.
Ben Jonson's Works. With Notes Critical and Explanatory, and a Biographical Memoir by WM. GIFFORD. Edit. by Col. CUNNINGHAM. 3 Vols.
Chapman's Works. Complete in Three Vols. Vol. I. contains the Plays complete, including doubtful ones; Vol. II., Poems and Minor Translations, with Introductory Essay by A. C. SWINBURNE; Vol. III., Translations of the Iliad and Odyssey.

DRAMATISTS, THE OLD, *continued*—
Crown 8vo, cloth extra, Vignette Portraits, 6s. per Volume.
Marlowe's Works. Including his Translations. Edited, with Notes and Introduction, by Col. CUNNINGHAM. One Vol.
Massinger's Plays. From the Text of WILLIAM GIFFORD. Edited by Col. CUNNINGHAM. One Vol.

Dyer. — The Folk-Lore of Plants. By Rev. T. F. THISELTON DYER, M.A. Crown 8vo, cloth extra, 7s. 6d. [*In preparation*.

Early English Poets. Edited, with Introductions and Annotations, by Rev. A. B. GROSART, D.D. Crown 8vo, cloth boards, 6s. per Volume.
Fletcher's (Giles, B.D.) Complete Poems. One Vol.
Davies' (Sir John) Complete Poetical Works. Two Vols.
Herrick's (Robert) Complete Collected Poems. Three Vols.
Sidney's (Sir Philip) Complete Poetical Works. Three Vols.
Herbert (Lord) of Cherbury's Poems. Edit., with Introd., by J. CHURTON COLLINS. Cr. 8vo, parchment, 8s.

Edgcumbe. — Zephyrus: A Holiday in Brazil and on the River Plate. By E. R. PEARCE EDGCUMBE. With 41 Illusts. Cr. 8vo, cl. extra, 5s.

Edwardes (Mrs. A.), Novels by:
A Point of Honour. Post 8vo, illustrated boards, 2s.
Archie Lovell. Crown 8vo, cloth extra, 3s. 6d.; post 8vo, illust. bds., 2s.

Eggleston.—Roxy: A Novel. By EDWARD EGGLESTON. Post 8vo, illust. boards, 2s.

Emanuel.—On Diamonds and Precious Stones: their History, Value, and Properties; with Simple Tests for ascertaining their Reality. By HARRY EMANUEL, F.R.G.S. With numerous Illustrations, tinted and plain. Crown 8vo, cloth extra, gilt, 6s.

Ewald (Alex. Charles, F.S.A.), Works by:
The Life and Times of Prince Charles Stuart, Count of Albany, commonly called the Young Pretender. From the State Papers and other Sources. New and Cheaper Edition, with a Portrait, crown 8vo, cloth extra, 7s. 6d.
Stories from the State Papers. With an Autotype Facsimile. Crown 8vo, cloth extra, 6s.
Studies Re-studied: Historical Sketches from Original Sources. Demy 8vo, cloth extra, 12s.

Eyes, Our: How to Preserve Them from Infancy to Old Age. By JOHN BROWNING, F.R.A.S., &c. Sixth Edition (Eleventh Thousand). With 58 Illustrations. Crown 8vo, cloth, 1s.

Fairholt.—Tobacco: Its History and Associations; with an Account of the Plant and its Manufacture, and its Modes of Use in all Ages and Countries. By F. W. FAIRHOLT, F.S.A. With upwards of 100 Illustrations by the Author. Crown 8vo, cloth extra, 6s.

Familiar Short Sayings of Great Men. By SAMUEL ARTHUR BENT, A.M. Fifth Edition, Revised and Enlarged. Crown 8vo, cloth extra, 7s. 6d.

Faraday (Michael), Works by:
Post 8vo, cloth extra, 4s. 6d. each.
The Chemical History of a Candle: Lectures delivered before a Juvenile Audience at the Royal Institution. Edited by WILLIAM CROOKES, F.C.S. With numerous Illustrations.
On the Various Forces of Nature, and their Relations to each other: Lectures delivered before a Juvenile Audience at the Royal Institution. Edited by WILLIAM CROOKES, F.C.S. With numerous Illustrations.

Farrer (James Anson), Works by:
Military Manners and Customs. Crown 8vo, cloth extra, 6s.
War: Three Essays, Reprinted from "Military Manners." Crown 8vo, 1s.; cloth, 1s. 6d.

Fin-Bec.—The Cupboard Papers: Observations on the Art of Living and Dining. By FIN-BEC. Post 8vo, cloth limp, 2s. 6d.

Fireworks, The Complete Art of Making; or, The Pyrotechnist's Treasury. By THOMAS KENTISH. With 267 Illustrations. A New Edition, Revised throughout and greatly Enlarged. Crown 8vo, cloth extra, 5s.

Fitzgerald (Percy), Works by:
The Recreations of a Literary Man; or, Does Writing Pay? With Recollections of some Literary Men, and a View of a Literary Man's Working Life. Cr. 8vo, cloth extra, 6s.
The World Behind the Scenes. Crown 8vo, cloth extra, 3s. 6d.
Little Essays: Passages from the Letters of CHARLES LAMB. Post 8vo, cloth limp, 2s. 6d.
A Day's Tour: A Journey through France and Belgium. With Sketches in facsimile of the Original Drawings. Crown 4to picture cover, 1s.

FITZGERALD (PERCY), *continued*—
Fatal Zero: A Homburg Diary. Cr. 8vo, cloth extra, 3s. 6d.

Post 8vo, illustrated boards, 2s. each.
Bella Donna. | Never Forgotten
The Second Mrs. Tillotson.
Polly.
Seventy-five Brooke Street.
The Lady of Brantome.

Fletcher's (Giles, B.D.) Complete Poems: Christ's Victorie in Heaven, Christ's Victorie on Earth, Christ's Triumph over Death, and Minor Poems. With Memorial-Introduction and Notes by the Rev. A. B. GROSART, D.D. Cr. 8vo, cloth bds., 6s.

Fonblanque.—Filthy Lucre: A Novel. By ALBANY DE FONBLANQUE. Post 8vo, illustrated boards, 2s.

Francillon (R. E.), Novels by:
Crown 8vo, cloth extra, 3s. 6d. each; post 8vo, illust. boards, 2s. each.
One by One. | A Real Queen.
Queen Cophetua. |
Olympia. Post 8vo, illust. boards, 2s.
Esther's Glove. Fcap. 8vo, 1s.

Frederic. — Seth's Brother's Wife: A Novel. By HAROLD FREDERIC. Two Vols., crown 8vo.

French Literature, History of By HENRY VAN LAUN. Complete in 3 Vols., demy 8vo, cl. bds., 7s. 6d. each.

Frere.—Pandurang Hari; or, Memoirs of a Hindoo. With a Preface by Sir H. BARTLE FRERE, G.C.S.I., &c. Crown 8vo, cloth extra, 3s. 6d.; post 8vo, illustrated boards, 2s.

Friswell.—One of Two: A Novel. By HAIN FRISWELL. Post 8vo, illustrated boards, 2s.

Frost (Thomas), Works by:
Crown 8vo, cloth extra, 3s. 6d. each.
Circus Life and Circus Celebrities.
The Lives of the Conjurers.
The Old Showmen and the Old London Fairs.

Fry's (Herbert) Royal Guide to the London Charities, 1887-8. Showing their Name, Date of Foundation, Objects, Income, Officials, &c. Published Annually. Cr. 8vo, cloth, 1s. 6d.

Gardening Books:
Post 8vo, 1s. each; cl. limp, 1s. 6d. each.
A Year's Work in Garden and Greenhouse: Practical Advice to Amateur Gardeners as to the Management of the Flower, Fruit, and Frame Garden. By GEORGE GLENNY.
Our Kitchen Garden: The Plants we Grow, and How we Cook Them. By TOM JERROLD.

GARDENING BOOKS, continued—
Post 8vo, 1s. each; cl. limp, 1s. 6d. each.
Household Horticulture: A Gossip about Flowers. By TOM and JANE JERROLD. Illustrated.
The Garden that Paid the Rent. By TOM JERROLD.

My Garden Wild, and What I Grew there. By F. G. HEATH. Crown 8vo, cloth extra, 5s.; gilt edges, 6s.

Garrett.—The Capel Girls: A Novel. By EDWARD GARRETT. Cr. 8vo, cl. ex., 3s. 6d.; post 8vo, illust. bds., 2s.

Gentleman's Magazine (The). One Shilling Monthly. In addition to the Articles upon subjects in Literature, Science, and Art, for which this Magazine has so high a reputation, "Science Notes," by W. MATTIEU WILLIAMS, F.R.A.S., and "Table Talk," by SYLVANUS URBAN, appear monthly.
*** Now ready, the Volume for JULY to DECEMBER, 1887, cloth extra, price 8s. 6d. Cases for binding, 2s. each.

Gentleman's Annual (The) for 1887. Consisting of one entire Novel, entitled The Golden Hoop: An After-Marriage Interlude. By T. W. SPEIGHT, Author of "The Mysteries of Heron Dyke." Demy 8vo, picture cover, 1s. [Nov. 10.

German Popular Stories. Collected by the Brothers GRIMM, and Translated by EDGAR TAYLOR. Edited, with an Introduction, by JOHN RUSKIN. With 22 Illustrations on Steel by GEORGE CRUIKSHANK. Square 8vo, cloth extra, 6s. 6d.; gilt edges, 7s. 6d.

Gibbon (Charles), Novels by:
Crown 8vo, cloth extra, 3s. 6d. each post 8vo, illustrated boards, 2s. each.
Robin Gray. | Braes of Yarrow.
What will the World Say? | A Heart's Problem.
In Honour Bound. | The Golden Shaft.
Queen of the Meadow. | Of High Degree.
The Flower of the Forest. | Fancy Free.
| Loving a Dream.
| A Hard Knot.

Post 8vo, illustrated boards, 2s. each.
For Lack of Gold.
For the King. | In Pastures Green.
In Love and War.
By Mead and Stream.
Heart's Delight. [Preparing.

Gilbert (William), Novels by:
Post 8vo, illustrated boards, 2s. each.
Dr. Austin's Guests.
The Wizard of the Mountain.
James Duke, Costermonger.

Gilbert (W. S.), Original Plays by: In Two Series, each complete in itself, price 2s. 6d. each.
The FIRST SERIES contains—The Wicked World—Pygmalion and Galatea—Charity—The Princess—The Palace of Truth—Trial by Jury.
The SECOND SERIES contains—Broken Hearts—Engaged—Sweethearts—Gretchen—Dan'l Druce—Tom Cobb—H.M.S. Pinafore—The Sorcerer—The Pirates of Penzance.

Eight Original Comic Operas. Written by W. S. GILBERT. Containing: The Sorcerer—H.M.S. "Pinafore" —The Pirates of Penzance—Iolanthe —Patience—Princess Ida—The Mikado—Trial by Jury. Demy 8vo, cloth limp, 2s. 6d.

Glenny.—A Year's Work in Garden and Greenhouse: Practical Advice to Amateur Gardeners as to the Management of the Flower, Fruit, and Frame Garden. By GEORGE GLENNY. Post 8vo, 1s.; cloth, 1s. 6d.

Godwin.—Lives of the Necromancers. By WILLIAM GODWIN. Post 8vo, limp, 2s.

Golden Library, The:
Square 16mo (Tauchnitz size), cloth limp, 2s. per Volume.
Bayard Taylor's Diversions of the Echo Club.
Bennett's (Dr. W. C.) Ballad History of England.
Bennett's (Dr.) Songs for Sailors.
Byron's Don Juan.
Godwin's (William) Lives of the Necromancers.
Holmes's Autocrat of the Breakfast Table. Introduction by SALA.
Holmes's Professor at the Breakfast Table.
Hood's Whims and Oddities. Complete. All the original Illustrations.
Irving's (Washington) Tales of a Traveller.
Jesse's (Edward) Scenes and Occupations of a Country Life.
Lamb's Essays of Elia. Both Series Complete in One Vol.
Leigh Hunt's Essays: A Tale for a Chimney Corner, and other Pieces. With Portrait, and Introduction by EDMUND OLLIER.
Mallory's (Sir Thomas) Mort d'Arthur: The Stories of King Arthur and of the Knights of the Round Table. Edited by B. MONTGOMERIE RANKING.

GOLDEN LIBRARY, THE, *continued* —
Square 16mo, 2s. per Volume.
Pascal's Provincial Letters. A New Translation, with Historical Introduction and Notes, by T. M'CRIE, D.D.
Pope's Poetical Works. Complete.
Rochefoucauld's Maxims and Moral Reflections. With Notes, and Introductory Essay by SAINTE-BEUVE.
St. Pierre's Paul and Virginia, and The Indian Cottage. Edited, with Life, by the Rev. E. CLARKE.

Golden Treasury of Thought,
The: An ENCYCLOPÆDIA OF QUOTATIONS from Writers of all Times and Countries. Selected and Edited by THEODORE TAYLOR. Crown 8vo, cloth gilt and gilt edges, 7s. 6d.

Graham. — The Professor's Wife: A Story. By LEONARD GRAHAM. Fcap. 8vo, picture cover, 1s.

Greeks and Romans, The Life of the, Described from Antique Monuments. By ERNST GUHL and W. KONER. Translated from the Third German Edition, and Edited by Dr. F. HUEFFER. 545 Illusts. New and Cheaper Edit., demy 8vo, cl. ex., 7s. 6d.

Greenaway (Kate) and Bret Harte.—The Queen of the Pirate Isle. By BRET HARTE. With 25 original Drawings by KATE GREENAWAY, Reproduced in Colours by E. EVANS. Sm. 4to, bds., 5s.

Greenwood (James), Works by:
Crown 8vo, cloth extra, 3s. 6d. each.
The Wilds of London.
Low-Life Deeps: An Account of the Strange Fish to be Found There.

Dick Temple: A Novel. Post 8vo, illustrated boards, 2s.

Guyot.—The Earth and Man; or, Physical Geography in its relation to the History of Mankind. By ARNOLD GUYOT. With Additions by Professors AGASSIZ, PIERCE, and GRAY; 12 Maps and Engravings on Steel, some Coloured, and copious Index. Crown 8vo, cloth extra, gilt, 4s. 6d.

Habberton (John), Author of "Helen's Babies," Novels by:
Post 8vo, illustrated boards, 2s. each; cloth limp, 2s. 6d. each.
Brueton's Bayou.
Country Luck.

Hair (The): Its Treatment in Health, Weakness, and Disease. Translated from the German of Dr. J. PINCUS. Crown 8vo, 12.; cloth, 1s. 6d.

Hake (Dr. Thomas Gordon), Poems by:
Crown 8vo, cloth extra, 6s. each.
New Symbols.
Legends of the Morrow.
The Serpent Play.

Maiden Ecstasy. Small 4to, cloth extra, 8s.

Hall.—Sketches of Irish Character. By Mrs. S. C. HALL. With numerous Illustrations on Steel and Wood by MACLISE, GILBERT, HARVEY, and G. CRUIKSHANK. Medium 8vo, cloth extra, gilt, 7s. 6d.

Halliday.—Every-day Papers. By ANDREW HALLIDAY. Post 8vo, illustrated boards, 2s.

Handwriting, The Philosophy of. With over 100 Facsimiles and Explanatory Text. By DON FELIX DE SALAMANCA. Post 8vo, cl. limp, 2s. 6d.

Hanky-Panky: A Collection of Very Easy Tricks, Very Difficult Tricks, White Magic, Sleight of Hand, &c. Edited by W. H. CREMER. With 200 Illusts. Crown 8vo, cloth extra, 4s. 6d.

Hardy (Lady Duffus). — Paul Wynter's Sacrifice: A Story. By Lady DUFFUS HARDY. Post 8vo, illust. boards, 2s.

Hardy (Thomas).—Under the Greenwood Tree. By THOMAS HARDY, Author of "Far from the Madding Crowd." With numerous Illustrations. Crown 8vo, cloth extra, 3s. 6d.; post 8vo, illustrated boards, 2s.

Harwood.—The Tenth Earl. By J. BERWICK HARWOOD. Post 8vo illustrated boards, 2s.

Haweis (Mrs. H. R.), Works by:
The Art of Dress. With numerous Illustrations. Small 8vo, illustrated cover, 1s.; cloth limp, 1s. 6d.
The Art of Beauty. New and Cheaper Edition. Crown 8vo, cloth extra, Coloured Frontispiece and Illusts. 6s.
The Art of Decoration. Square 8vo, handsomely bound and profusely Illustrated, 10s. 6d.
Chaucer for Children: A Golden Key. With Eight Coloured Pictures and numerous Woodcuts. New Edition, small 4to, cloth extra, 6s.
Chaucer for Schools. Demy 8vo, cloth limp, 2s. 6d.

Haweis (Rev. H. R.).—American Humorists: WASHINGTON IRVING, OLIVER WENDELL HOLMES, JAMES RUSSELL LOWELL, ARTEMUS WARD, MARK TWAIN, and BRET HARTE. By Rev. H. R. HAWEIS, M.A. Cr. 8vo, 6s.

BOOKS PUBLISHED BY

Hawthorne.—Tanglewood Tales for Girls and Boys. By NATHANIEL HAWTHORNE. With numerous fine Illustrations by G. WHARTON EDWARDS. Large 4to, cloth extra, 10s. 6d.

Hawthorne (Julian), Novels by. Crown 8vo, cloth extra, 3s. 6d. each; post 8vo, illustrated boards, 2s. each.

Garth. | Sebastian Strome.
Ellice Quentin. | Dust.
Prince Saroni's Wife.
Fortune's Fool. | Beatrix Randolph.

Crown 8vo, cloth extra, 3s. 6d. each.
Miss Cadogna.
Love—or a Name.

Mrs. Gainsborough's Diamonds. Fcap. 8vo, illustrated cover, 1s.

Hays.—Women of the Day: A Biographical Dictionary of Notable Contemporaries. By FRANCES HAYS. Crown 8vo, cloth extra, 5s.

Heath (F. G.).— My Garden Wild, and What I Grew There. By FRANCIS GEORGE HEATH, Author of "The Fern World," &c. Crown 8vo, cloth extra, 5s.; cl. gilt, gilt edges. 6s.

Helps (Sir Arthur), Works by: Post 8vo, cloth limp, 2s. 6d. each.
Animals and their Masters.
Social Pressure.

Ivan de Biron: A Novel. Crown 8vo, cloth extra, 3s. 6d.; post 8vo, illustrated boards, 2s.

Herman.—One Traveller Returns: A Romance. By HENRY HERMAN and D. CHRISTIE MURRAY. Crown 8vo, cloth extra, 6s.

Herrick's (Robert) Hesperides, Noble Numbers, and Complete Collected Poems. With Memorial-Introduction and Notes by the Rev. A. B. GROSART, D.D., Steel Portrait, Index of First Lines, and Glossarial Index, &c. Three Vols., crown 8vo, cloth, 18s.

Hesse-Wartegg (Chevalier Ernst von), Works by:
Tunis: The Land and the People. With 22 Illustrations. Crown 8vo, cloth extra, 3s. 6d.
The New South-West: Travelling Sketches from Kansas, New Mexico, Arizona, and Northern Mexico. With 100 fine Illustrations and Three Maps. Demy 8vo, cloth extra, 14s. [*In preparation.*

Herbert.—The Poems of Lord Herbert of Cherbury. Edited, with Introduction, by J. CHURTON COLLINS. Crown 8vo, bound in parchment, 8s.

Hindley (Charles), Works by: Crown 8vo, cloth extra, 3s. 6d. each.
Tavern Anecdotes and Sayings: Including the Origin of Signs, and Reminiscences connected with Taverns, Coffee Houses, Clubs, &c. With Illustrations.
The Life and Adventures of a Cheap Jack. By One of the Fraternity. Edited by CHARLES HINDLEY.

Hoey.—The Lover's Creed. By Mrs. CASHEL HOEY. With Frontispiece by P. MACNAB. Post 8vo, illustrated boards, 2s.

Holmes (O. Wendell), Works by:
The Autocrat of the Breakfast-Table. Illustrated by J. GORDON THOMSON. Post 8vo, cloth limp, 2s. 6d.—Another Edition in smaller type, with an Introduction by G. A. SALA. Post 8vo, cloth limp, 2s.
The Professor at the Breakfast-Table; with the Story of Iris. Post 8vo, cloth limp, 2s.

Holmes. — The Science of Voice Production and Voice Preservation: A Popular Manual for the Use of Speakers and Singers. By GORDON HOLMES, M.D. With Illustrations. Crown 8vo, 1s.; cloth, 1s. 6d.

Hood (Thomas):
Hood's Choice Works, in Prose and Verse. Including the Cream of the COMIC ANNUALS. With Life of the Author, Portrait, and 200 Illustrations. Crown 8vo, cloth extra, 7s. 6d.
Hood's Whims and Oddities. Complete. With all the original Illustrations. Post 8vo, cloth limp, 2s.

Hood (Tom), Works by:
From Nowhere to the North Pole: A Noah's Arkæological Narrative. With 25 Illustrations by W. BRUNTON and E. C. BARNES. Square crown 8vo, cloth extra, gilt edges, 6s.
A Golden Heart: A Novel. Post 8vo, illustrated boards, 2s.

Hook's (Theodore) Choice Humorous Works, including his Ludicrous Adventures, Bons Mots, Puns and Hoaxes. With a New Life of the Author, Portraits, Facsimiles, and Illusts. Cr. 8vo, cl. extra, gilt, 7s. 6d.

Hooper.—The House of Raby: A Novel. By Mrs. GEORGE HOOPER. Post 8vo, illustrated boards, 2s.

Hopkins—"'Twixt Love and Duty:" A Novel. By TIGHE HOPKINS. Crown 8vo, cloth extra, 6s.; post 8vo illustrated boards, 2s.

Horne.—Orion: An Epic Poem, in Three Books. By RICHARD HENGIST HORNE. With Photographic Portrait from a Medallion by SUMMERS. Tenth Edition, crown 8vo, cloth extra, 7s.

Howell.—Conflicts of Capital and Labour, Historically and Economically considered: Being a History and Review of the Trade Unions of Great Britain. By GEO. HOWELL M.P. Crown 8vo, cloth extra, 7s. 6d.

Hunt (Mrs. Alfred), Novels by: Crown 8vo, cloth extra, 3s. 6d. each; post 8vo, illustrated boards, 2s. each.
Thornicroft's Model.
The Leaden Casket.
Self-Condemned.
That other Person.

Hunt.—Essays by Leigh Hunt. A Tale for a Chimney Corner, and other Pieces. With Portrait and Introduction by EDMUND OLLIER. Post 8vo, cloth limp, 2s.

Hydrophobia: an Account of M. PASTEUR'S System. Containing a Translation of all his Communications on the Subject, the Technique of his Method, and the latest Statistical Results. By RENAUD SUZOR, M.B., C.M. Edin., and M.D. Paris, Commissioned by the Government of the Colony of Mauritius to study M. PASTEUR'S new Treatment in Paris. With 7 Illustrations. Crown 8vo, cloth extra, 6s.

Indoor Paupers. By ONE OF THEM. Crown 8vo, 1s.; cloth, 1s. 6d.

Ingelow.—Fated to be Free: A Novel. By JEAN INGELOW. Crown 8vo, cloth extra, 3s. 6d.; post 8vo, illustrated boards, 2s.

Irish Wit and Humour, Songs of. Collected and Edited by A. PERCEVAL GRAVES. Post 8vo, cloth limp, 2s. 6d.

Irving—Tales of a Traveller. By WASHINGTON IRVING. Post 8vo, cloth limp, 2s.

Janvier.—Practical Keramics for Students. By CATHERINE A. JANVIER. Crown 8vo, cloth extra, 6s.

Jay (Harriett), Novels by: Post 8vo, illustrated boards, 2s. each.
The Dark Colleen.
The Queen of Connaught.

Jefferies (Richard), Works by: Crown 8vo, cloth extra, 6s. each.
The Life of the Fields.
The Open Air.

Nature near London. Crown 8vo, cloth extra, 6s.; post 8vo, cloth limp, 2s. 6d.

Jennings (H. J.), Works by:
Curiosities of Criticism. Post 8vo, cloth limp, 2s. 6d.
Lord Tennyson: A Biographical Sketch. With a Photograph-Portrait. Crown 8vo, cloth extra, 6s.

Jerrold (Tom), Works by: Post 8vo, 1s. each; cloth, 1s. 6d. each.
The Garden that Paid the Rent.
Household Horticulture: A Gossip about Flowers. Illustrated.
Our Kitchen Garden: The Plants we Grow, and How we Cook Them.

Jesse.—Scenes and Occupations of a Country Life. By EDWARD JESSE. Post 8vo, cloth limp, 2s.

Jeux d'Esprit. Collected and Edited by HENRY S. LEIGH. Post 8vo, cloth limp, 2s. 6d.

Jones (Wm., F.S.A.), Works by: Crown 8vo, cloth extra, 7s. 6d. each.
Finger-Ring Lore: Historical, Legendary, and Anecdotal. With over Two Hundred Illustrations.
Credulities, Past and Present; including the Sea and Seamen, Miners, Talismans, Word and Letter Divination Exorcising and Blessing of Animals, Birds, Eggs, Luck, &c. With an Etched Frontispiece.
Crowns and Coronations: A History of Regalia in all Times and Countries. With One Hundred Illustrations.

Jonson's (Ben) Works. With Notes Critical and Explanatory, and a Biographical Memoir by WILLIAM GIFFORD. Edited by Colonel CUNNINGHAM. Three Vols., crown 8vo, cloth extra, 18s.; or separately, 6s. each.

Josephus, The Complete Works of. Translated by WHISTON. Containing both "The Antiquities of the Jews" and "The Wars of the Jews." Two Vols., 8vo, with 52 Illustrations and Maps, cloth extra, gilt, 14s.

Kempt.—Pencil and Palette: Chapters on Art and Artists. By ROBERT KEMPT. Post 8vo, cloth limp, 2s. 6d.

Kershaw.—Colonial Facts and Fictions: Humorous Sketches. By MARK KERSHAW. Post 8vo, illustrated boards, 2s.; cloth, 2s. 6d.

King (R. Ashe), Novels by:
Crown 8vo, cloth extra, 3s. 6d. each; post 8vo, illustrated boards, 2s. each.
A Drawn Game.
"The Wearing of the Green."

Kingsley (Henry), Novels by:
Oakshott Castle. Post 8vo, illustrated boards, 2s.
Number Seventeen. Crown 8vo, cloth extra, 3s. 6d.

Knight.—The Patient's Vade Mecum: How to get most Benefit from Medical Advice. By WILLIAM KNIGHT, M.R.C.S., and EDWARD KNIGHT, L.R.C.P. Crown 8vo, 1s.; cloth, 1s. 6d.

Lamb (Charles):
Lamb's Complete Works, in Prose and Verse, reprinted from the Original Editions, with many Pieces hitherto unpublished. Edited, with Notes and Introduction, by R. H. SHEPHERD. With Two Portraits and Facsimile of Page of the "Essay on Roast Pig." Cr. 8vo, cl. extra, 7s. 6d.
The Essays of Elia. Complete Edition. Post 8vo, cloth extra, 2s.
Poetry for Children, and Prince Dorus. By CHARLES LAMB. Carefully reprinted from unique copies. Small 8vo, cloth extra, 5s.
Little Essays: Sketches and Characters. By CHARLES LAMB. Selected from his Letters by PERCY FITZGERALD. Post 8vo, cloth limp, 2s. 6d.

Lane's Arabian Nights, &c.:
The Thousand and One Nights: commonly called, in England, "THE ARABIAN NIGHTS' ENTERTAINMENTS." A New Translation from the Arabic, with copious Notes, by EDWARD WILLIAM LANE. Illustrated by many hundred Engravings on Wood, from Original Designs by WM. HARVEY. A New Edition, from a Copy annotated by the Translator, edited by his Nephew, EDWARD STANLEY POOLE. With a Preface by STANLEY LANE-POOLE. Three Vols., demy 8vo, cloth extra, 7s. 6d. each.
Arabian Society in the Middle Ages: Studies from "The Thousand and One Nights." By EDWARD WILLIAM LANE, Author of "The Modern Egyptians," &c. Edited by STANLEY LANE-POOLE. Cr. 8vo, cloth extra, 6s.

Lares and Penates; or, The Background of Life. By FLORENCE CADDY. Crown 8vo, cloth extra, 6s.

Larwood (Jacob), Works by:
The Story of the London Parks. With Illustrations. Crown 8vo, cloth extra, 3s. 6d.

Post 8vo, cloth limp, 2s. 6d. each.
Forensic Anecdotes.
Theatrical Anecdotes.

Life in London; or, The History of Jerry Hawthorn and Corinthian Tom. With the whole of CRUIKSHANK'S Illustrations, in Colours, after the Originals. Crown 8vo, cloth extra, 7s. 6d.

Linskill.—In Exchange for a Soul. By MARY LINSKILL, Author of "The Haven Under the Hill," &c. Three Vols., crown 8vo.

Linton (E. Lynn), Works by:
Post 8vo, cloth limp, 2s. 6d. each.
Witch Stories.
The True Story of Joshua Davidson.
Ourselves: Essays on Women.

Crown 8vo, cloth extra, 3s. 6d. each; post 8vo, illustrated boards, 2s. each.
Patricia Kemball.
The Atonement of Leam Dundas.
The World Well Lost.
Under which Lord?
With a Silken Thread.
The Rebel of the Family.
"My Love!" | Ione.

Paston Carew, Millionaire and Miser. Crown 8vo, cloth, 3s. 6d.

Longfellow's Poetical Works. Carefully Reprinted from the Original Editions. With numerous fine Illustrations on Steel and Wood. Crown 8vo, cloth extra, 7s. 6d.

Long Life, Aids to: A Medical, Dietetic, and General Guide in Health and Disease. By N. E. DAVIES, L.R.C.P. Crown 8vo, 2s.; cloth limp, 2s. 6d.

Lucy.—Gideon Fleyce: A Novel. By HENRY W. LUCY. Crown 8vo, cl. ex., 3s. 6d.; post 8vo, illust. bds., 2s.

Lusiad (The) of Camoens. Translated into English Spenserian Verse by ROBERT FFRENCH DUFF. Demy 8vo, with Fourteen full-page Plates, cloth boards, 18s.

Macalpine. — Teresa Itasca, and other Stories. By AVERY MACALPINE. Crown 8vo, bound in canvas, 2s. 6d.

McCarthy (Justin, M.P.), Works by:

A History of Our Own Times, from the Accession of Queen Victoria to the General Election of 1880. Four Vols. demy 8vo, cloth extra, 12s. each.—Also a POPULAR EDITION, in Four Vols. cr. 8vo, cl. extra, 6s. each.—And a JUBILEE EDITION, with an Appendix of Events to the end of 1886, complete in Two Vols., square 8vo, cloth extra, 7s. 6d. each.

A Short History of Our Own Times. One Vol., crown 8vo, cloth extra, 6s.

History of the Four Georges. Four Vols. demy 8vo, cloth extra, 12s. each. [Vol. I. *now ready.*

Crown 8vo, cloth extra, 3s. 6d. each; post 8vo, illustrated boards, 2s. each.
Dear Lady Disdain.
The Waterdale Neighbours.
A Fair Saxon.
Miss Misanthrope.
Donna Quixote.
The Comet of a Season.
Maid of Athens.
Camiola: A Girl with a Fortune.

Post 8vo, illustrated boards, 2s. each.
Linley Rochford.
My Enemy's Daughter.

"The Right Honourable:" A Romance of Society and Politics. By JUSTIN MCCARTHY, M.P., and Mrs. CAMPBELL-PRAED. New and Cheaper Edition, crown 8vo, cloth extra, 6s.

McCarthy (Justin H., M.P.), Works by:

An Outline of the History of Ireland, from the Earliest Times to the Present Day. Cr. 8vo, 1s.; cloth, 1s. 6d.

Ireland since the Union: Sketches of Irish History from 1798 to 1886. Crown 8vo, cloth extra, 6s.

The Case for Home Rule. Crown 8vo, cloth extra, 5s.

England under Gladstone, 1880-85. Second Edition, revised. Crown 8vo, cloth extra, 6s.

Doom! An Atlantic Episode. Crown 8vo, 1s.; cloth, 1s. 6d.

Our Sensation Novel. Edited by JUSTIN H. MCCARTHY. Crown 8vo, 1s.; cloth, 1s. 6d.

Hafiz in London. Choicely printed. Small 8vo, gold cloth, 3s. 6d.

MacDonald.—Works of Fancy and Imagination. By GEORGE MACDONALD, LL.D. Ten Volumes, in handsome cloth case, 21s. Vol. I. WITHIN AND WITHOUT. THE HIDDEN LIFE.—Vol. 2. THE DISCIPLE. THE GOSPEL WOMEN. A BOOK OF SONNETS, ORGAN SONGS.—Vol. 3. VIOLIN SONGS. SONGS OF THE DAYS AND NIGHTS. A BOOK OF DREAMS. ROADSIDE POEMS. POEMS FOR CHILDREN. Vol. 4. PARABLES. BALLADS. SCOTCH SONGS.—Vols. 5 and 6. PHANTASTES: A Faerie Romance.—Vol. 7. THE PORTENT.—Vol. 8. THE LIGHT PRINCESS. THE GIANT'S HEART. SHADOWS.—Vol. 9. CROSS PURPOSES. THE GOLDEN KEY. THE CARASOYN. LITTLE DAYLIGHT.—Vol. 10. THE CRUEL PAINTER. THE WOW O' RIVVEN. THE CASTLE. THE BROKEN SWORDS. THE GRAY WOLF. UNCLE CORNELIUS.

The Volumes are also sold separately in Grolier-pattern cloth, 2s. 6d. each.

Macdonell.—Quaker Cousins: A Novel. By AGNES MACDONELL. Crown 8vo, cloth extra, 3s. 6d.; post 8vo, illustrated boards, 2s.

Macgregor. — Pastimes and Players. Notes on Popular Games. By ROBERT MACGREGOR. Post 8vo, cloth limp, 2s. 6d.

Mackay.—Interludes and Undertones; or, Music at Twilight. By CHARLES MACKAY, LL.D. Crown 8vo, cloth extra, 6s.

Maclise Portrait-Gallery (The) of Illustrious Literary Characters; with Memoirs—Biographical, Critical, Bibliographical, and Anecdotal—illustrative of the Literature of the former half of the Present Century. By WILLIAM BATES, B.A. With 85 Portraits printed on an India Tint. Crown 8vo, cloth extra, 7s. 6d.

Macquoid (Mrs.), Works by:
Square 8vo, cloth extra, 10s. 6d. each.
In the Ardennes. With 50 fine Illustrations by THOMAS R. MACQUOID.
Pictures and Legends from Normandy and Brittany. With numerous Illusts. by THOMAS R. MACQUOID
About Yorkshire. With 67 Illustrations by T. R. MACQUOID.

Crown 8vo, cloth extra, 7s. 6d. each.
Through Normandy. With 90 Illustrations by T. R. MACQUOID.
Through Brittany. With numerous Illustrations by T. R. MACQUOID.

Post 8vo, illustrated boards, 2s. each.
The Evil Eye, and other Stories.
Lost Rose.

BOOKS PUBLISHED BY

Magician's Own Book (The): Performances with Cups and Balls, Eggs, Hats, Handkerchiefs, &c. All from actual Experience. Edited by W. H. CREMER. With 200 Illustrations. Crown 8vo, cloth extra, 4s. 6d.

Magic Lantern (The), and its Management: including full Practical Directions for producing the Limelight, making Oxygen Gas, and preparing Lantern Slides. By T. C. HEPWORTH. With 10 Illustrations. Crown 8vo, 1s.; cloth, 1s. 6d.

Magna Charta. An exact Facsimile of the Original in the British Museum, printed on fine plate paper, 3 feet by 2 feet, with Arms and Seals emblazoned in Gold and Colours. 5s.

Mallock (W. H.), Works by:
The New Republic; or, Culture, Faith and Philosophy in an English Country House. Post 8vo, cloth limp, 2s. 6d.; Cheap Edition, illustrated boards, 2s.
The New Paul and Virginia; or, Positivism on an Island. Post 8vo, cloth limp, 2s. 6d.
Poems. Small 4to, in parchment, 8s.
Is Life worth Living? Crown 8vo, cloth extra, 6s.

Mallory's (Sir Thomas) Mort d'Arthur: The Stories of King Arthur and of the Knights of the Round Table. Edited by B. MONTGOMERIE RANKING. Post 8vo, cloth limp, 2s.

Mark Twain, Works by:
The Choice Works of Mark Twain. Revised and Corrected throughout by the Author. With Life, Portrait, and numerous Illustrations. Crown 8vo, cloth extra, 7s. 6d.
The Innocents Abroad; or, The New Pilgrim's Progress: Being some Account of the Steamship "Quaker City's" Pleasure Excursion to Europe and the Holy Land. With 234 Illustrations. Crown 8vo, cloth extra, 7s. 6d.—Cheap Edition (under the title of "MARK TWAIN'S PLEASURE TRIP"), post 8vo, illust. boards, 2s.
Roughing It, and The Innocents at Home. With 200 Illustrations by F. A. FRASER. Cr. 8vo, cl. ex., 7s. 6d.
The Gilded Age. By MARK TWAIN and CHARLES DUDLEY WARNER. With 212 Illustrations by T. COPPIN Crown 8vo, cloth extra, 7s. 6d.
The Adventures of Tom Sawyer With 111 Illustrations. Crown 8vo, cloth extra, 7s. 6d.—Cheap Edition, post 8vo, illustrated boards, 2s.
The Prince and the Pauper. With nearly 200 Illustrations. Crown 8vo, cloth extra, 7s. 6d.

MARK TWAIN'S WORKS, *continued*—
A Tramp Abroad. With 314 Illusts. Cr. 8vo, cloth extra, 7s. 6d.—Cheap Edition, post 8vo, illust. bds., 2s.
The Stolen White Elephant, &c. Crown 8vo, cloth extra, 6s.; post 8vo, illustrated boards, 2s.
Life on the Mississippi. With about 300 Original Illustrations. Crown 8vo, cloth extra, 7s. 6d.—Cheap Edition, post 8vo, illustrated boards, 2s.
The Adventures of Huckleberry Finn. With 174 Illustrations by E. W. KEMBLE. Crown 8vo, cloth extra, 7s. 6d.—Cheap Edition, post 8vo, illustrated boards, 2s.
Mark Twain's Library of Humour. With numerous Illustrations. Crown 8vo, cloth extra, 7s. 6d. [*Preparing.*

Marlowe's Works. Including his Translations. Edited, with Notes and Introductions, by Col. CUNNINGHAM. Crown 8vo, cloth extra, 6s.

Marryat (Florence), Novels by:
Crown 8vo, cloth extra, 3s. 6d. each; post 8vo, illustrated boards, 2s. each.
Open! Sesame! | Written in Fire.
Post 8vo, illustrated boards, 2s. each.
A Harvest of Wild Oats.
A Little Stepson.
Fighting the Air.

Massinger's Plays. From the Text of WILLIAM GIFFORD. Edited by Col. CUNNINGHAM. Crown 8vo, cloth extra, 6s.

Masterman.—Half a Dozen Daughters: A Novel. By J. MASTERMAN. Post 8vo, illustrated boards, 2s.

Matthews.—A Secret of the Sea, &c. By BRANDER MATTHEWS. Post 8vo, illustrated boards, 2s.; cloth, 2s. 6d.

Mayfair Library, The:
Post 8vo, cloth limp, 2s. 6d. per Volume.
A Journey Round My Room. By XAVIER DE MAISTRE. Translated by HENRY ATTWELL.
Quips and Quiddities. Selected by W. DAVENPORT ADAMS.
The Agony Column of "The Times," from 1800 to 1870. Edited, with an Introduction, by ALICE CLAY.
Melancholy Anatomised: A Popular Abridgment of "Burton's Anatomy of Melancholy."
Gastronomy as a Fine Art. By BRILLAT-SAVARIN.
The Speeches of Charles Dickens.
Literary Frivolities, Fancies, Follies, and Frolics. By W. T. DOBSON.
Poetical Ingenuities and Eccentricities. Selected and Edited by W. T. DOBSON.

MAYFAIR LIBRARY, continued—
Post 8vo, cloth limp, 2s. 6d. per Vol.
The Cupboard Papers. By FIN-BEC.
Original Plays by W. S. GILBERT.
FIRST SERIES. Containing: The Wicked World — Pygmalion and Galatea — Charity — The Princess — The Palace of Truth — Trial by Jury.
Original Plays by W. S. GILBERT SECOND SERIES. Containing: Broken Hearts — Engaged — Sweethearts — Gretchen — Dan'l Druce — Tom Cobb — H.M.S. Pinafore — The Sorcerer — The Pirates of Penzance.
Songs of Irish Wit and Humour. Collected and Edited by A. PERCEVAL GRAVES.
Animals and their Masters. By Sir ARTHUR HELPS.
Social Pressure. By Sir A. HELPS.
Curiosities of Criticism. By HENRY J. JENNINGS.
The Autocrat of the Breakfast-Table By OLIVER WENDELL HOLMES. Illustrated by J. GORDON THOMSON.
Pencil and Palette. By ROBERT KEMPT.
Little Essays: Sketches and Characters. By CHAS. LAMB. Selected from his Letters by PERCY FITZGERALD.
Forensic Anecdotes; or, Humour and Curiosities of the Law and Men of Law. By JACOB LARWOOD.
Theatrical Anecdotes. By JACOB LARWOOD.
Jeux d'Esprit. Edited by HENRY S. LEIGH.
True History of Joshua Davidson. By E. LYNN LINTON.
Witch Stories. By E. LYNN LINTON.
Ourselves: Essays on Women. By E. LYNN LINTON.
Pastimes and Players. By ROBERT MACGREGOR.
The New Paul and Virginia. By W. H. MALLOCK.
New Republic. By W. H. MALLOCK.
Puck on Pegasus. By H. CHOLMONDELEY-PENNELL.
Pegasus Re-Saddled. By H. CHOLMONDELEY-PENNELL. Illustrated by GEORGE DU MAURIER.
Muses of Mayfair. Edited by H. CHOLMONDELEY-PENNELL.
Thoreau: His Life and Aims. By H. A. PAGE.
Puniana. By the Hon. HUGH ROWLEY.
More Puniana. By the Hon. HUGH ROWLEY.
The Philosophy of Handwriting. By DON FELIX DE SALAMANCA.
By Stream and Sea. By WILLIAM SENIOR.
Old Stories Re-told. By WALTER THORNBURY.
Leaves from a Naturalist's Note-Book. By Dr. ANDREW WILSON.

Mayhew.—London Characters and the Humorous Side of London Life. By HENRY MAYHEW. With numerous Illustrations. Crown 8vo, cloth extra, 3s. 6d.

Medicine, Family.—One Thousand Medical Maxims and Surgical Hints, for Infancy, Adult Life, Middle Age, and Old Age. By N. E. DAVIES, L.R.C.P. Lond. Cr. 8vo, 1s.; cl., 1s. 6d.

Merry Circle (The): A Book of New Intellectual Games and Amusements. By CLARA BELLEW. With numerous Illustrations. Crown 8vo, cloth extra, 4s. 6d.

Mexican Mustang (On a), through Texas, from the Gulf to the Rio Grande. A New Book of American Humour. By ALEX. E. SWEET and J. ARMOY KNOX, Editors of "Texas Siftings." With 265 Illusts. Cr. 8vo, cloth extra, 7s. 6d.

Middlemass (Jean), Novels by
Post 8vo, illustrated boards, 2s. each.
Touch and Go. | Mr. Dorillion.

Miller. — Physiology for the Young; or, The House of Life: Human Physiology, with its application to the Preservation of Health. For Classes and Popular Reading. With numerous Illusts. By Mrs. F. FENWICK MILLER. Small 8vo, cloth limp, 2s. 6d.

Milton (J. L.), Works by:
Sm. 8vo, 1s. each; cloth ex., 1s. 6d. each.
The Hygiene of the Skin. A Concise Set of Rules for the Management of the Skin; with Directions for Diet, Wines, Soaps, Baths, &c.
The Bath in Diseases of the Skin.
The Laws of Life, and their Relation to Diseases of the Skin.

Molesworth (Mrs.).—Hathercourt Rectory. By Mrs. MOLESWORTH, Author of "The Cuckoo Clock," &c. Cr. 8vo, cl. extra, 4s. 6d.

Moncrieff.—The Abdication; or, Time Tries All. An Historical Drama. By W D. SCOTT-MONCRIEFF. With Seven Etchings by JOHN PETTIE, R.A., W. Q. ORCHARDSON, R.A., J. MACWHIRTER, A.R.A., COLIN HUNTER, A.R.A., R. MACBETH, A.R.A., and TOM GRAHAM, R.S.A. Large 4to, bound in buckram, 21s.

Murray (D. Christie), Novels by. Crown 8vo, cloth extra, 3s. 6d. each; post 8vo, illustrated boards, 2s. each.
A Life's Atonement. | A Model Father.
Joseph's Coat. | Coals of Fire.
By the Gate of the Sea.
Val Strange. | Hearts.

BOOKS PUBLISHED BY

MURRAY (D. C.), *continued*—
Crown 8vo, cloth extra, 3s. 6d.; post 8vo, illustrated boards, 2s. each.
The Way of the World.
A Bit of Human Nature.
First Person Singular.
Cynic Fortune.
Old Blazer's Hero. With Three Illustrations by A. MCCORMICK. Crown 8vo, cloth extra, 6s.
One Traveller Returns. By D. CHRISTIE MURRAY and HENRY HERMAN. Cr. 8vo, cl. ex. 6s.

North Italian Folk. By Mrs. COMYNS CARR. Illust. by RANDOLPH CALDECOTT. Sq. 8vo, cl. ex., 7s. 6d.

Novelists. — Half-Hours with the Best Novelists of the Century: Choice Readings from the finest Novels. Edited, with Critical and Biographical Notes, by H. T. MACKENZIE BELL. Crown 8vo, cl. ex., 3s. 6d. [*Preparing*.

Nursery Hints: A Mother's Guide in Health and Disease. By N. E. DAVIES, L.R.C.P. Cr.8vo. 1s.; cl., 1s.6d.

O'Connor.—Lord Beaconsfield: A Biography. By T. P. O'CONNOR, M.P. Sixth Edition, with a New Preface, bringing the work down to the Death of Lord Beaconsfield. Crown 8vo, cloth extra, 7s. 6d.

O'Hanlon. — The Unforeseen: A Novel. By ALICE O'HANLON. New and Cheaper Edition. Post 8vo, illustrated boards, 2s.

Oliphant (Mrs.) Novels by:
Whiteladies. With Illustrations by ARTHUR HOPKINS and H. WOODS. Crown 8vo, cloth extra, 3s. 6d.; post 8vo, illustrated boards, 2s.
Crown 8vo, cloth extra, 4s. 6d. each.
The Primrose Path.
The Greatest Heiress in England.

O'Reilly.—Phœbe's Fortunes: A Novel. With Illustrations by HENRY TUCK. Post 8vo, illustrated boards, 2s.

O'Shaughnessy (A.), Works by:
Songs of a Worker. Fcap. 8vo, cloth extra, 7s. 6d.
Music and Moonlight. Fcap. 8vo, cloth extra, 7s. 6d.
Lays of France. Cr.8vo, cl. ex.,10s. 6d.

Ouida, Novels by. Crown 8vo, cloth extra, 5s. each; post 8vo, illustrated boards, 2s. each.
Held in Bondage. | Tricotrin.
Strathmore. | Puck.
Chandos. | Folle Farine.
Under Two Flags. | Two Little Wooden
Cecil Castle- | Shoes.
maine's Gage. | A Dog of Flanders.
Idalia. | Pascarel.

OUIDA, *continued*—
Crown 8vo, cloth extra, 5s. each; post 8vo, illustrated boards, 2s. each.
Signa. | Ariadne. | A Village Com-
In a Winter City. | mune.
Friendship. | Wanda.
Moths. | Bimbi. Frescoes. [Ine.
Pipistrello. | Princess Naprax-
In Maremma. | Othmar.
Wisdom, Wit, and Pathos, selected from the Works of OUIDA by F. SYDNEY MORRIS. Sm.cr.8vo,cl.ex.,5s.

Page (H. A.), Works by:
Thoreau: His Life and Aims: A Study. With Portrait. Post 8vo,cl,limp,2s.6d.
Lights on the Way: Some Tales within a Tale. By the late J. H. ALEXANDER, B.A. Edited by H. A. PAGE. Crown 8vo, cloth extra, 6s.
Animal Anecdotes. Arranged on a New Principle. Cr. 8vo, cl. extra, 5s.

Parliamentary Elections and Electioneering in the Old Days (A History of). Showing the State of Political Parties and Party Warfare at the Hustings and in the House of Commons from the Stuarts to Queen Victoria. Illustrated from the original Political Squibs, Lampoons, Pictorial Satires, and Popular Caricatures of the Time. By JOSEPH GREGO, Author of "Rowlandson and his Works," "The Life of Gillray," &c. A New Edition, crown 8vo, cloth extra, with Coloured Frontispiece and 100 Illustrations, 7s. 6d. [*Preparing*.

Pascal's Provincial Letters. A New Translation, with Historical Introduction and Notes, by T. M'CRIE, D.D. Post 8vo, cloth limp, 2s.

Patient's (The) Vade Mecum: How to get most Benefit from Medical Advice. By W. KNIGHT, M.R.C.S., and E. KNIGHT, L.R.C.P. Cr.8vo, 1s.; cl. 1/6.

Paul Ferroll:
Post 8vo, illustrated boards, 2s. each.
Paul Ferroll: A Novel.
Why Paul Ferroll Killed his Wife.

Payn (James), Novels by.
Crown 8vo, cloth extra, 3s. 6d. each; post 8vo, illustrated boards, 2s. each.
Lost Sir Massingberd.
The Best of Husbands.
Walter's Word.
Less Black than we're Painted.
By Proxy. | High Spirits.
Under One Roof.
A Confidential Agent.
Some Private Views.
A Grape from a Thorn.
For Cash Only. | From Exile.
The Canon's Ward.
The Talk of the Town.

CHATTO & WINDUS, PICCADILLY. 19

Payn (James), continued—
Post 8vo, illustrated boards, 2s. each.
Kit: A Memory. | Carlyon's Year.
A Perfect Treasure.
Bentinck's Tutor. Murphy's Master.
What He Cost Her.
Fallen Fortunes. | Halves.
A County Family. | At Her Mercy.
A Woman's Vengeance.
Cecil's Tryst.
The Clyffards of Clyffe.
The Family Scapegrace.
The Foster Brothers.| Found Dead.
Gwendoline's Harvest.
Humorous Stories.
Like Father, Like Son.
A Marine Residence.
Married Beneath Him.
Mirk Abbey. | Not Wooed, but Won.
Two Hundred Pounds Reward.

In Peril and Privation: Stories of Marine Adventure Re-told. A Book for Boys. With numerous Illustrations. Crown 8vo, cloth gilt, 6s.

Holiday Tasks: Being Essays written in Vacation Time. Crown 8vo, 6s.

Glow-worm Tales. Cheaper Edition, crown 8vo, cloth extra, 3s. 6d.

Paul.—Gentle and Simple. By MARGARET AGNES PAUL. With a Frontispiece by HELEN PATERSON. Cr. 8vo, cloth extra, 3s. 6d.; post 8vo, illustrated boards, 2s.

Pears.—The Present Depression in Trade: Its Causes and Remedies. Being the "Pears" Prize Essays (of One Hundred Guineas). By EDWIN GOADBY and WILLIAM WATT. With an Introductory Paper by Prof. LEONE LEVI, F.S.A., F.S.S. Demy 8vo, 1s.

Pennell (H. Cholmondeley), Works by:
Post 8vo, cloth limp, 2s. 6d. each.
Puck on Pegasus. With Illustrations.
Pegasus Re-Saddled. With Ten full-page Illusts. by G. DU MAURIER.
The Muses of Mayfair. Vers de Société, Selected and Edited by H. C. PENNELL.

Phelps (E. Stuart), Works by:
Post 8vo, 1s. each; cl. limp, 1s. 6d. each.
Beyond the Gates. By the Author of "The Gates Ajar."
An Old Maid's Paradise.
Burglars in Paradise.

Jack the Fisherman. With Twenty-two Illustrations by C. W. REED. Cr. 8vo, picture cover, 1s.; cl. 1s. 6d.

Pirkis (C. L.), Novels by:
Trooping with Crows. Fcap. 8vo, picture cover, 1s.
Lady Lovelace. Post 8vo, illustrated boards, 2s. [Preparing.

Planché (J. R.), Works by:
The Pursuivant of Arms; or, Heraldry Founded upon Facts. With Coloured Frontispiece and 200 Illustrations. Cr. 8vo, cloth extra, 7s. 6d.
Songs and Poems, from 1819 to 1879. Edited, with an Introduction, by his Daughter, Mrs. MACKARNESS. Crown 8vo, cloth extra, 6s.

Plutarch's Lives of Illustrious Men. Translated from the Greek, with Notes Critical and Historical, and a Life of Plutarch, by JOHN and WILLIAM LANGHORNE. Two Vols., 8vo, cloth extra, with Portraits, 10s. 6d.

Poe (Edgar Allan):—
The Choice Works, in Prose and Poetry, of EDGAR ALLAN POE. With an Introductory Essay by CHARLES BAUDELAIRE, Portrait and Facsimiles. Crown 8vo, cl. extra, 7s. 6d.
The Mystery of Marie Roget, and other Stories. Post 8vo. illust.bds.,2s.

Pope's Poetical Works. Complete in One Vol. Post 8vo, cl. limp, 2s.

Praed (Mrs. Campbell-).—"The Right Honourable:" A Romance of Society and Politics. By Mrs. CAMPBELL-PRAED and JUSTIN MCCARTHY, M.P. Cr. 8vo, cloth extra, 6s.

Price (E. C.), Novels by:
Crown 8vo, cloth extra, 3s. 6d. each; post 8vo, illustrated boards, 2s. each.
Valentina. | The Foreigners.
Mrs. Lancaster's Rival.
Gerald. Post 8vo, illust. boards, 2s.

Princess Olga—Radna; or, The Great Conspiracy of 1881. By the Princess OLGA. Cr. 8vo, cl. ex., 6s.

Proctor (Richd. A.), Works by:
Flowers of the Sky. With 55 Illusts. Small crown 8vo, cloth extra, 4s. 6d.
Easy Star Lessons. With Star Maps for Every Night in the Year, Drawings of the Constellations, &c. Crown 8vo, cloth extra, 6s.
Familiar Science Studies. Crown 8vo, cloth extra, 7s. 6d.
Saturn and Its System. New and Revised Edition, with 13 Steel Plates. Demy 8vo, cloth extra, 10s. 6d.
The Great Pyramid: Observatory, Tomb, and Temple. With Illustrations. Crown 8vo, cloth extra, 6s.
Mysteries of Time and Space. With Illusts. Cr. 8vo, cloth extra, 7s. 6d.
The Universe of Suns, and other Science Gleanings. With numerous Illusts. Cr. 8vo, cloth extra, 7s. 6d.
Wages and Wants of Science Workers. Crown 8vo, 1s. 6d.

BOOKS PUBLISHED BY

Rabelais' Works. Faithfully Translated from the French, with variorum Notes, and numerous characteristic Illustrations by GUSTAVE DORÉ. Crown 8vo, cloth extra, 7s. 6d.

Rambosson.—Popular Astronomy. By J. RAMBOSSON, Laureate of the Institute of France. Translated by C. B. PITMAN. Crown 8vo, cloth gilt, numerous Illusts., and a beautifully executed Chart of Spectra, 7s. 6d.

Reade (Charles), Novels by:
Cr. 8vo, cloth extra, illustrated, 3s. 6d. each; post 8vo, illust. bds., 2s. each.
Peg Woffington. Illustrated by S. L. FILDES, A.R.A.
Christie Johnstone. Illustrated by WILLIAM SMALL.
It is Never Too Late to Mend. Illustrated by G. J. PINWELL.
The Course of True Love Never did run Smooth. Illustrated by HELEN PATERSON.
The Autobiography of a Thief; Jack of all Trades; and James Lambert. Illustrated by MATT STRETCH.
Love me Little, Love me Long. Illustrated by M. ELLEN EDWARDS.
The Double Marriage. Illust. by Sir JOHN GILBERT, R.A., and C. KEENE.
The Cloister and the Hearth. Illustrated by CHARLES KEENE.
Hard Cash. Illust. by F. W. LAWSON.
Griffith Gaunt. Illustrated by S. L. FILDES, A.R.A., and WM. SMALL.
Foul Play. Illust. by DU MAURIER.
Put Yourself in His Place. Illustrated by ROBERT BARNES.
A Terrible Temptation. Illustrated by EDW. HUGHES and A. W. COOPER.
The Wandering Heir. Illustrated by H. PATERSON, S. L. FILDES, A.R.A., C. GREEN, and H. WOODS, A.R.A.
A Simpleton. Illustrated by KATE CRAUFORD. [COULDERY.
A Woman-Hater. Illust. by THOS.
Singleheart and Doubleface: A Matter-of-fact Romance. Illustrated by P. MACNAB.
Good Stories of Men and other Animals. Illustrated by E. A. ABBEY, PERCY MACQUOID, and JOSEPH NASH.
The Jilt, and other Stories. Illustrated by JOSEPH NASH.
Readiana. With a Steel-plate Portrait of CHARLES READE.

Reader's Handbook (The) of Allusions, References, Plots, and Stories. By the Rev. Dr. BREWER. Fifth Edition, revised throughout, with a New Appendix, containing a COMPLETE ENGLISH BIBLIOGRAPHY. Cr. 8vo, 1,400 pages, cloth extra, 7s. 6d.

Red Spider: A Romance. By the Author of "John Herring," &c. Cr. 8vo, cloth extra, 3s. 6d.

Rice (Portrait of James).— Specially etched by DANIEL A. WEHRSCHMIDT for the New Library Edition of BESANT and RICE's Novels. A few Proofs before Letters have been taken on Japanese paper, size 15¾ × 10 in. Price 5s. each.

Richardson. — A Ministry of Health, and other Papers. By BENJAMIN WARD RICHARDSON, M.D., &c. Crown 8vo, cloth extra, 6s.

Riddell (Mrs. J. H.), Novels by:
Crown 8vo, cloth extra, 3s. 6d. each; post 8vo, illustrated boards, 2s. each.
Her Mother's Darling.
The Prince of Wales's Garden Party.
Weird Stories.
Post 8vo, illustrated boards, 2s. each.
The Uninhabited House.
Fairy Water.
The Mystery in Palace Gardens.

Rimmer (Alfred), Works by:
Square 8vo, cloth gilt, 10s. 6d. each.
Our Old Country Towns. With over 50 Illustrations.
Rambles Round Eton and Harrow. With 50 Illustrations.
About England with Dickens. With 58 Illustrations by ALFRED RIMMER and C. A. VANDERHOOF.

Robinson Crusoe: A beautiful reproduction of Major's Edition, with 37 Woodcuts and Two Steel Plates by GEORGE CRUIKSHANK, choicely printed. Crown 8vo, cloth extra, 7s. 6d.

Robinson (F. W.), Novels by:
Crown 8vo, cloth extra, 3s. 6d. each; post 8vo, illustrated boards, 2s. each.
Women are Strange.
The Hands of Justice.

Robinson (Phil), Works by:
Crown 8vo, cloth extra, 7s. 6d. each.
The Poets' Birds.
The Poets' Beasts.
The Poets and Nature: Reptiles, Fishes, and Insects. [Preparing.

Rochefoucauld's Maxims and Moral Reflections. With Notes, and an Introductory Essay by SAINTE-BEUVE. Post 8vo, cloth limp, 2s.

Roll of Battle Abbey, The; or, A List of the Principal Warriors who came over from Normandy with William the Conqueror, and Settled in this Country, A.D. 1066-7. With the principal Arms emblazoned in Gold and Colours. Handsomely printed, 5s.

CHATTO & WINDUS, PICCADILLY. 21

Rowley (Hon. Hugh), Works by:
Post 8vo, cloth limp, 2s. 6d. each.
Puniana: Riddles and Jokes. With numerous Illustrations.
More Puniana. Profusely Illustrated.

Runciman (James), Stories by:
Post 8vo, illustrated boards, 2s. each; cloth limp, 2s. 6d each.
Skippers and Shellbacks.
Grace Balmaign's Sweetheart.
Schools and Scholars.

Russell (W. Clark), Works by:
Crown 8vo, cloth extra, 6s. each; post 8vo, illustrated boards, 2s. each.
Round the Galley-Fire.
On the Fo'k'sle Head.
In the Middle Watch.
Crown 8vo, cloth extra, 6s. each.
A Voyage to the Cape.
A Book for the Hammock.
The Frozen Pirate, the New Serial Novel by W. CLARK RUSSELL, Author of "The Wreck of the *Grosvenor*," began in "Belgravia" for July, and will be continued till January next. One Shilling, Monthly. Illustrated.

Sala.—Gaslight and Daylight.
By GEORGE AUGUSTUS SALA. Post 8vo, illustrated boards, 2s.

Sanson.—Seven Generations of Executioners: Memoirs of the Sanson Family (1688 to 1847). Edited by HENRY SANSON. Cr. 8vo, cl. ex. 3s. 6d.

Saunders (John), Novels by:
Crown 8vo, cloth extra, 3s. 6d. each; post 8vo, illustrated boards, 2s. each.
Bound to the Wheel.
Guy Waterman. | Lion in the Path.
The Two Dreamers.
One Against the World. Post 8vo, illustrated boards, 2s.

Saunders (Katharine), Novels by. Cr. 8vo, cloth extra, 3s. 6d. each; post 8vo, illustrated boards, 2s. each.
Joan Merryweather.
Margaret and Elizabeth.
The High Mills.
Heart Salvage. | Sebastian.
Gideon's Rock. Crown 8vo, cloth extra, 3s. 6d.

Science Gossip: An Illustrated Medium of Interchange for Students and Lovers of Nature. Edited by J. E. TAYLOR, F.L.S., &c. Devoted to Geology, Botany, Physiology, Chemistry, Zoology, Microscopy, Telescopy, Physiography, &c. Price 4d. Monthly; or 5s. per year, post free. Vols. I. to XIV. may be had at 7s. 6d. each; and Vols. XV. to XXIII. (1887), at 5s. each. Cases for Binding, 1s. 6d. each.

"Secret Out" Series, The:
Cr. 8vo, cl. ex., Illusts., 4s. 6d. each.
The Secret Out: One Thousand Tricks with Cards, and other Recreations; with Entertaining Experiments in Drawing-room or "White Magic." By W. H. CREMER. 300 Illusts.
The Art of Amusing: A Collection of Graceful Arts, Games, Tricks, Puzzles, and Charades By FRANK BELLEW. With 300 Illustrations.
Hanky-Panky: Very Easy Tricks Very Difficult Tricks, White Magic Sleight of Hand. Edited by W. H. CREMER. With 200 Illustrations.
The Merry Circle: A Book of New Intellectual Games and Amusements. By CLARA BELLEW. Many Illusts.
Magician's Own Book: Performances with Cups and Balls, Eggs, Hats, Handkerchiefs, &c. All from actual Experience. Edited by W. H. CREMER. 200 Illustrations.

Senior.—By Stream and Sea.
By W. SENIOR. Post 8vo, cl. limp, 2s. 6d.

Seven Sagas (The) of Prehistoric Man. By JAMES H. STODDART, Author of "The Village Life." Crown 8vo, cloth extra, 6s.

Shakespeare:
The First Folio Shakespeare.—MR. WILLIAM SHAKESPEARE's Comedies, Histories, and Tragedies. Published according to the true Originall Copies. London, Printed by ISAAC IAGGARD and ED. BLOUNT. 1623.—A Reproduction of the extremely rare original, in reduced facsimile, by a photographic process—ensuring the strictest accuracy in every detail. Small 8vo, half-Roxburghe, 7s. 6d.
The Lansdowne Shakespeare. Beautifully printed in red and black, in small but very clear type. With engraved facsimile of DROESHOUT's Portrait. Post 8vo, cloth extra, 7s. 6d.
Shakespeare for Children: Tales from Shakespeare. By CHARLES and MARY LAMB. With numerous Illustrations, coloured and plain, by J. MOYR SMITH. Cr. 4to, cl. gilt, 6s.
The Handbook of Shakespeare Music. Being an Account of 350 Pieces of Music, set to Words taken from the Plays and Poems of Shakespeare, the compositions ranging from the Elizabethan Age to the Present Time. By ALFRED ROFFE. 4to, half-Roxburghe, 7s.
A Study of Shakespeare. By ALGERNON CHARLES SWINBURNE. Crown 8vo, cloth extra, 8s.

Shelley.—The Complete Works
In Verse and Prose of Percy Bysshe Shelley. Edited, Prefaced and Annotated by RICHARD HERNE SHEPHERD. Five Vols., crown 8vo, cloth boards, 3s. 6d. each.

Poetical Works, in Three Vols.
Vol. I. An Introduction by the Editor; The Posthumous Fragments of Margaret Nicholson; Shelley's Correspondence with Stockdale; The Wandering Jew (the only complete version); Queen Mab, with the Notes; Alastor, and other Poems; Rosalind and Helen; Prometheus Unbound; Adonais, &c.
Vol. II. Laon and Cythna (as originally published, instead of the emasculated "Revolt of Islam"); The Cenci; Julian and Maddalo (from Shelley's manuscript); Swellfoot the Tyrant (from the copy in the Dyce Library at South Kensington); The Witch of Atlas; Epipsychidion; Hellas.
Vol. III. Posthumous Poems, published by Mrs. SHELLEY in 1824 and 1839; The Masque of Anarchy (from Shelley's manuscript); and other Pieces not brought together in the ordinary editions.

Prose Works, in Two Vols.
Vol. I. The Two Romances of Zastrozzi and St. Irvyne; the Dublin and Marlow Pamphlets; A Refutation of Deism; Letters to Leigh Hunt, and some Minor Writings and Fragments.
Vol. II. The Essays; Letters from Abroad; Translations and Fragments, Edited by Mrs. SHELLEY, and first published in 1840, with the addition of some Minor Pieces of great interest and rarity, including one recently discovered by Professor DOWDEN. With a Bibliography of Shelley and an exhaustive Index of the Prose Works.

. Also a LARGE-PAPER EDITION, to be had in SETS only, at 52s. 6d. for the Five Volumes.

Sheridan :—
Sheridan's Complete Works, with Life and Anecdotes. Including his Dramatic Writings, printed from the Original Editions, his Works in Prose and Poetry, Translations, Speeches, Jokes, Puns, &c. With a Collection of Sheridaniana. Crown 8vo, cloth extra, gilt, with 10 full-page Tinted Illustrations, 7s. 6d.
Sheridan's Comedies: The Rivals, and The School for Scandal. Edited, with an Introduction and Notes to each Play, and a Biographical Sketch of Sheridan, by BRANDER MATTHEWS. With Decorative Vignettes and 10 full-page Illusts. Demy 8vo, half-parchment, 12s. 6d.

Sidney's (Sir Philip) Complete
Poetical Works, including all those in "Arcadia." With Portrait, Memorial-Introduction, Notes, &c., by the Rev. A. B. GROSART, D.D. Three Vols., crown 8vo, cloth boards, 18s.

Signboards: Their History.
With Anecdotes of Famous Taverns and Remarkable Characters. By JACOB LARWOOD and JOHN CAMDEN HOTTEN. Crown 8vo, cloth extra, with 100 Illustrations, 7s. 6d.

Sims (George R.), Works by :
How the Poor Live. With 60 Illusts. by FRED. BARNARD. Large 4to, 1s.
Post 8vo, illustrated boards, 2s. each; cloth limp, 2s. 6d. each.
Rogues and Vagabonds.
The Ring o' Bells.
Mary Jane's Memoirs.

Sister Dora: A Biography. By MARGARET LONSDALE. Popular Edition, Revised, with additional Chapter, a New Dedication and Preface, and Four Illustrations. Sq. 8vo, picture cover, 4d.; cloth, 6d.

Sketchley.—A Match in the Dark. By ARTHUR SKETCHLEY. Post 8vo, illustrated boards, 2s.

Slang Dictionary, The: Etymological, Historical, and Anecdotal. Crown 8vo, cloth extra, gilt, 6s. 6d.

Smith (J. Moyr), Works by :
The Prince of Argolis: A Story of the Old Greek Fairy Time. Small 8vo, cloth extra, with 130 Illusts., 3s. 6d.
Tales of Old Thule. With numerous Illustrations. Cr. 8vo, cloth gilt, 6s.
The Wooing of the Water Witch: A Northern Oddity. With numerous Illustrations. Small 8vo, cl. ex., 6s.

Society in London. By A FOREIGN RESIDENT. Crown 8vo, 1s.; cloth, 1s. 6d.

Society in Paris: The Upper Ten Thousand. By Count PAUL VASILI. Trans. by RAPHAEL LEDOS DE BEAUFORT Cr. 8vo. cl. ex.. 6s. [*Preparing.*

Spalding.—Elizabethan Demonology: An Essay in Illustration of the Belief in the Existence of Devils, and the Powers possessed by Them. By T. A. SPALDING, LL.B. Cr. 8vo, cl. ex., 5s.

Spanish Legendary Tales. By Mrs. S. G. C. MIDDLEMORE, Author of "Round a Posada Fire." Crown 8vo, cloth extra, 6s.

Speight (T. W.), Novels by:
The Mysteries of Heron Dyke. With a Frontispiece by M. ELLEN EDWARDS. Crown 8vo, cloth extra, 3s. 6d.; post 8vo, illustrated bds., 2s.
A Barren Title. Cr. 8vo, 1s.; cl., 1s.6d.
Wife or No Wife? Cr. 8vo, picture cover, 1s.; cloth, 1s. 6d.
The Golden Hoop. Demy 8vo, 1s.

Spenser for Children. By M. H. TOWRY. With Illustrations by WALTER J. MORGAN. Crown 4to, with Coloured Illustrations, cloth gilt, 6s.

Starting in Life: Hints for Parents on the Choice of a Profession for their Sons. By FRANCIS DAVENANT, M.A. Post 8vo, 1s.; cloth limp, 1s. 6d.

Staunton.—Laws and Practice of Chess; Together with an Analysis of the Openings, and a Treatise on End Games. By HOWARD STAUNTON. Edited by ROBERT B. WORMALD. New Edition, small cr. 8vo, cloth extra, 5s.

Stedman (E. C.), Works by:
Victorian Poets. Thirteenth Edition, revised and enlarged. Crown 8vo, cloth extra, 9s.
The Poets of America. Crown 8vo, cloth extra, 9s.

Sterndale.—The Afghan Knife: A Novel. By ROBERT ARMITAGE STERNDALE. Cr. 8vo, cloth extra, 3s. 6d.; post 8vo, illustrated boards, 2s.

Stevenson (R. Louis), Works by:
Travels with a Donkey in the Cevennes. Sixth Ed. Frontispiece by W. CRANE. Post 8vo, cl. limp, 2s. 6d.
An Inland Voyage. With Front. by W. CRANE. Post 8vo, cl. lp., 2s. 6d.
Familiar Studies of Men and Books. Second Edit. Crown 8vo, cl. ex., 6s.
New Arabian Nights. Crown 8vo, cl. extra, 6s.; post 8vo, illust. bds., 2s.
The Silverado Squatters. With Frontispiece. Cr. 8vo, cloth extra, 6s. Cheap Edition, post 8vo, picture cover, 1s.; cloth, 1s. 6d.
Prince Otto: A Romance. Fourth Edition. Crown 8vo, cloth extra, 6s.; post 8vo, illustrated boards, 2s.
The Merry Men, and other Tales and Fables. Cr. 8vo, cl. ex., 6s.
Underwoods: Poems. Post 8vo, cl. ex. 6s.
Memories and Portraits. Fcap. 8vo, buckram extra, 6s.
Virginibus Puerisque, and other Papers. A New Edition, Revised. Fcap. 8vo, buckram extra, 6s.

St. John.—A Levantine Family. By BAYLE ST. JOHN. Post 8vo, illustrated boards, 2s.

Stoddard.—Summer Cruising in the South Seas. By CHARLES WARREN STODDARD. Illust. by WALLIS MACKAY. Crown 8vo, cl. extra, 3s. 6d.

Stories from Foreign Novelists. With Notices of their Lives and Writings. By HELEN and ALICE ZIMMERN. Frontispiece. Crown 8vo, cloth extra, 3s. 6d.; post 8vo, illust. bds., 2s.

St. Pierre.—Paul and Virginia, and The Indian Cottage. By BERNARDIN ST. PIERRE. Edited, with Life, by Rev. E. CLARKE. Post 8vo, cl. lp., 2s.

Strutt's Sports and Pastimes of the People of England; including the Rural and Domestic Recreations, May Games, Mummeries, Shows, &c., from the Earliest Period to the Present Time. With 140 Illustrations. Edited by WM. HONE. Cr. 8vo, cl. extra, 7s. 6d.

Suburban Homes (The) of London: A Residential Guide to Favourite London Localities, their Society, Celebrities, and Associations. With Notes on their Rental, Rates, and House Accommodation. With Map of Suburban London. Cr. 8vo, cl. ex., 7s. 6d.

Swift's Choice Works, in Prose and Verse. With Memoir, Portrait, and Facsimiles of the Maps in the Original Edition of "Gulliver's Travels." Cr. 8vo, cloth extra, 7s. 6d.

Swinburne (Algernon C.), Works by:
Selections from the Poetical Works of Algernon Charles Swinburne. Fcap. 8vo, cloth extra, 6s.
Atalanta in Calydon. Crown 8vo, 6s.
Chastelard. A Tragedy. Cr. 8vo, 7s.
Poems and Ballads. FIRST SERIES. Fcap. 8vo, 9s. Cr. 8vo, same price.
Poems and Ballads. SECOND SERIES. Fcap. 8vo, 9s. Cr. 8vo, same price.
Notes on Poems and Reviews. 8vo, 1s.
Songs before Sunrise. Cr. 8vo, 10s. 6d.
Bothwell: A Tragedy. Cr. 8vo, 12s. 6d.
George Chapman: An Essay. Cr. 8vo, 7s.
Songs of Two Nations. Cr. 8vo, 6s.
Essays and Studies. Crown 8vo, 12s.
Erechtheus: A Tragedy. Cr. 8vo, 6s.
Note of an English Republican on the Muscovite Crusade. 8vo, 1s.
Note on Charlotte Bronte. Cr. 8vo, 6s.
A Study of Shakespeare. Cr. 8vo, 8s.
Songs of the Springtides. Cr. 8vo, 6s.
Studies in Song. Crown 8vo, 7s.
Mary Stuart: A Tragedy. Cr. 8vo, 8s.
Tristram of Lyonesse, and other Poems. Crown 8vo, 9s.
A Century of Roundels. Small 4to, 8s.
A Midsummer Holiday, and other Poems. Crown 8vo, 7s.
Marino Faliero: A Tragedy. Cr. 8vo, 6s.
A Study of Victor Hugo. Cr. 8vo, 6s.
Miscellanies. Crown 8vo, 12s.
Locrine: A Tragedy. Crown 8vo, 6s.

Symonds.—Wine, Women, and Song: Mediæval Latin Students' Songs. Now first translated into English Verse, with Essay by J. ADDINGTON SYMONDS. Small 8vo, parchment, 6s.

Syntax's (Dr.) Three Tours: In Search of the Picturesque, in Search of Consolation, and in Search of a Wife. With the whole of ROWLANDSON's droll page Illustrations in Colours and a Life of the Author by J. C. HOTTEN. Med. 8vo, cloth extra, 7s. 6d.

Taine's History of English Literature. Translated by HENRY VAN LAUN. Four Vols., small 8vo, cloth boards, 30s.—POPULAR EDITION, Two Vols., crown 8vo, cloth extra, 15s.

Taylor's (Bayard) Diversions of the Echo Club: Burlesques of Modern Writers. Post 8vo, cl. limp, 2s.

Taylor (Dr. J. E., F.L.S.), Works by. Crown 8vo, cloth ex., 7s. 6d. each.
The Sagacity and Morality of Plants: A Sketch of the Life and Conduct of the Vegetable Kingdom. Coloured Frontispiece and 100 Illust.
Our Common British Fossils, and Where to Find Them: A Handbook for Students. With 331 Illustrations.
The Playtime Naturalist: A Book for every Home. With about 300 Illustrations. Crown 8vo, cloth extra, 6s. [*Preparing.*

Taylor's (Tom) Historical Dramas: "Clancarty," "Jeanne Darc,""'Twixt Axe and Crown," "The Fool's Revenge," "Arkwright's Wife," "Anne Boleyn," "Plot and Passion." One Vol., cr. 8vo, cloth extra, 7s. 6d.
*** The Plays may also be had separately, at 1s. each.

Tennyson (Lord): A Biographical Sketch. By H. J. JENNINGS. With a Photograph-Portrait. Crown 8vo, cloth extra, 6s.

Thackerayana: Notes and Anecdotes. Illustrated by Hundreds of Sketches by WILLIAM MAKEPEACE THACKERAY, depicting Humorous Incidents in his School-life, and Favourite Characters in the books of his every-day reading. With Coloured Frontispiece. Cr. 8vo, cl. extra, 7s. 6d.

Thomas (Bertha), Novels by: Crown 8vo, cloth extra, 3s. 6d. each post 8vo, illustrated boards, 2s. each.
Cressida. | Proud Maisie.
The Violin-Player.

Thomas (M.).—A Fight for Life: A Novel. By W. MOY THOMAS. Post 8vo, illustrated boards, 2s.

Thomson's Seasons and Castle of Indolence. With a Biographical and Critical Introduction by ALLAN CUNNINGHAM, and over 50 fine Illustrations on Steel and Wood. Crown 8vo, cloth extra, gilt edges, 7s. 6d.

Thornbury (Walter), Works by Haunted London. Edited by EDWARD WALFORD, M.A. With Illustrations by F. W. FAIRHOLT, F.S.A. Crown 8vo, cloth extra, 7s. 6d.
The Life and Correspondence of J. M. W. Turner. Founded upon Letters and Papers furnished by his Friends and fellow Academicians. With numerous Illusts. in Colours, facsimiled from Turner's Original Drawings. Cr. 8vo, cl. extra, 7s. 6d.
Old Stories Re-told. Post 8vo, cloth limp, 2s. 6d.
Tales for the Marines. Post 8vo, illustrated boards, 2s.

Timbs (John), Works by: Crown 8vo, cloth extra, 7s. 6d. each.
The History of Clubs and Club Life in London. With Anecdotes of its Famous Coffee-houses, Hostelries, and Taverns. With many Illusts.
English Eccentrics and Eccentricities: Stories of Wealth and Fashion, Delusions, Impostures, and Fanatic Missions, Strange Sights and Sporting Scenes, Eccentric Artists, Theatrical Folk, Men of Letters, &c. With nearly 50 Illusts.

Trollope (Anthony), Novels by Crown 8vo, cloth extra, 3s. 6d. each; post 8vo, illustrated boards, 2s. each.
The Way We Live Now.
Kept in the Dark.
Frau Frohmann. | Marion Fay.
Mr. Scarborough's Family.
The Land-Leaguers.
Post 8vo, illustrated boards, 2s. each.
The Golden Lion of Granpere.
John Caldigate. | American Senator

Trollope (Frances E.), Novels by Crown 8vo, cloth extra, 3s. 6d. each; post 8vo, illustrated boards, 2s. each.
Like Ships upon the Sea.
Mabel's Progress. | Anne Furness.

Trollope (T. A.).—Diamond Cut Diamond, and other Stories. By T. ADOLPHUS TROLLOPE. Post 8vo, illustrated boards, 2s.

Trowbridge.—Farnell's Folly: A Novel. By J. T. TROWBRIDGE. Post 8vo, illustrated boards, 2s.

Turgenieff. — Stories from Foreign Novelists. By IVAN TURGENIEFF, and others. Cr. 8vo, cloth extra, 3s. 6d.; post 8vo, illustrated boards, 2s.

CHATTO & WINDUS, PICCADILLY. 25

Tytler (C. C. Fraser-). — Mistress Judith: A Novel. By C. C. FRASER-TYTLER. Cr. 8vo, cloth extra, 3s. 6d.; post 8vo, illust. boards, 2s.

Tytler (Sarah), Novels by:
Crown 8vo, cloth extra, 3s. 6d. each; post 8vo, illustrated boards, 2s. each.
What She Came Through.
The Bride's Pass.
Saint Mungo's City.
Beauty and the Beast.
Noblesse Oblige.
Lady Bell.

Crown 8vo, cloth extra, 3s. 6d. each.
Citoyenne Jacqueline. Illustrated by A. B. HOUGHTON.
The Huguenot Family. With Illusts.
Buried Diamonds.

Disappeared. With Six Illustrations by P. MACNAB. Crown 8vo, cloth extra, 6s.

Van Laun.— History of French Literature. By H. VAN LAUN. Three Vols., demy 8vo, cl. bds., 7s. 6d. each.

Villari.— A Double Bond: A Story. By LINDA VILLARI. Fcap. 8vo, picture cover, 1s.

Walford (Edw., M.A.), Works by:
The County Families of the United Kingdom. Containing Notices of the Descent, Birth, Marriage, Education, &c., of more than 12000, distinguished Heads of Families, their Heirs Apparent or Presumptive, the Offices they hold or have held, their Town and Country Addresses, Clubs, &c. Twenty-seventh Annual Edition, for 1887, cloth gilt, 50s.

The Shilling Peerage (1887). Containing an Alphabetical List of the House of Lords, Dates of Creation, Lists of Scotch and Irish Peers, Addresses, &c. 32mo, cloth, 1s. Published annually.

The Shilling Baronetage (1887). Containing an Alphabetical List of the Baronets of the United Kingdom, short Biographical Notices, Dates of Creation, Addresses, &c. 32mo, cloth, 1s.

The Shilling Knightage (1887). Containing an Alphabetical List of the Knights of the United Kingdom, short Biographical Notices, Dates of Creation, Addresses,&c. 32mo,cl.,1s.

The Shilling House of Commons (1887). Containing a List of all the Members of Parliament, their Town and Country Addresses, &c. New Edition, embodying the results of the recent General Election. 32mo, cloth, 1s. Published annually.

WALFORD'S (EDW.) WORKS, *continued*—
The Complete Peerage, Baronetage, Knightage, and House of Commons (1887). In One Volume, royal 32mo, cloth extra, gilt edges, 5s.

Haunted London. By WALTER THORNBURY. Edited by EDWARD WALFORD, M.A. With Illustrations by F. W. FAIRHOLT, F.S.A. Crown 8vo, cloth extra, 7s. 6d.

Walton and Cotton's Complete Angler; or, The Contemplative Man's Recreation; being a Discourse of Rivers, Fishponds, Fish and Fishing, written by IZAAK WALTON; and Instructions how to Angle for a Trout or Grayling in a clear Stream, by CHARLES COTTON. With Original Memoirs and Notes by Sir HARRIS NICOLAS, and 61 Copperplate Illustrations. Large crown 8vo, cloth antique, 7s. 6d.

Walt Whitman, Poems by.
Selected and edited, with an Introduction, by WILLIAM M. ROSSETTI. A New Edition, with a Steel Plate Portrait. Crown 8vo, printed on handmade paper and bound in buckram, 6s.

Wanderer's Library, The:
Crown 8vo, cloth extra, 3s. 6d. each.
Wanderings in Patagonia; or, Life among the Ostrich-Hunters. By JULIUS BEERBOHM. Illustrated.
Camp Notes: Stories of Sport and Adventure in Asia, Africa, and America. By FREDERICK BOYLE.
Savage Life. By FREDERICK BOYLE.
Merrie England in the Olden Time. By GEORGE DANIEL. With Illustrations by ROBT. CRUIKSHANK.
Circus Life and Circus Celebrities. By THOMAS FROST.
The Lives of the Conjurers. By THOMAS FROST.
The Old Showmen and the Old London Fairs. By THOMAS FROST.
Low-Life Deeps. An Account of the Strange Fish to be found there. By JAMES GREENWOOD.
The Wilds of London. By JAMES GREENWOOD.
Tunis: The Land and the People. By the Chevalier de HESSE-WARTEGG. With 22 Illustrations.
The Life and Adventures of a Cheap Jack. By One of the Fraternity. Edited by CHARLES HINDLEY.
The World Behind the Scenes. By PERCY FITZGERALD.
Tavern Anecdotes and Sayings: Including the Origin of Signs, and Reminiscences connected with Taverns, Coffee Houses, Clubs, &c. By CHARLES HINDLEY. With Illusts.
The Genial Showman: Life and Adventures of Artemus Ward. By E. P. HINGSTON. With a Frontispiece.

Wanderer's Library, The, *continued—*
The Story of the London Parks. By Jacob Larwood. With Illusts.
London Characters. By Henry Mayhew. Illustrated.
Seven Generations of Executioners: Memoirs of the Sanson Family (1688 to 1847). Edited by Henry Sanson.
Summer Cruising in the South Seas. By C. Warren Stoddard. Illustrated by Wallis Mackay.

Warner.—A Roundabout Journey. By Charles Dudley Warner, Author of "My Summer in a Garden." Crown 8vo, cloth extra, 6s.

Warrants, &c.:—
Warrant to Execute Charles I. An exact Facsimile, with the Fifty-nine Signatures, and corresponding Seals. Carefully printed on paper to imitate the Original, 22 in. by 14 in. Price 2s.
Warrant to Execute Mary Queen of Scots. An exact Facsimile, including the Signature of Queen Elizabeth, and a Facsimile of the Great Seal. Beautifully printed on paper to imitate the Original MS. Price 2s.
Magna Charta. An exact Facsimile of the Original Document in the British Museum, printed on fine plate paper, nearly 3 feet long by 2 feet wide, with the Arms and Seals emblazoned in Gold and Colours. 5s.
The Roll of Battle Abbey; or, A List of the Principal Warriors who came over from Normandy with William the Conqueror, and Settled in this Country, A.D. 1066-7. With the principal Arms emblazoned in Gold and Colours. Price 5s.

Wayfarer, The: Journal of the Society of Cyclists. Published at short intervals. The Numbers for October, 1886, and for January, May, and October, 1887, are now ready.

Weather, How to Foretell the, with the Pocket Spectroscope. By F. W. Cory, M.R.C.S. Eng., F.R.Met. Soc., &c. With 10 Illustrations. Crown 8vo, 1s.; cloth, 1s. 6d.

Westropp.—Handbook of Pottery and Porcelain; or, History of those Arts from the Earliest Period. By Hodder M. Westropp. With numerous Illustrations, and a List of Marks. Crown 8vo, cloth limp, 4s. 6d.

Whist. — How to Play Solo Whist: Its Method and Principles Explained, and its Practice Demonstrated. With Illustrative Specimen Hands, and a Revised and Augmented Code of Laws. By Abraham S. Wilks and Charles F. Pardon. Crown 8vo, cloth extra, 3s. 6d. [*Shortly.*

Whistler's (Mr.) "Ten o'Clock." Uniform with his "Whistler v. Ruskin: Art and Art Critics." Cr.8vo,1s. [*Shortly.*

Williams (W. Mattieu, F.R.A.S.), Works by:
Science Notes. See the Gentleman's Magazine. 1s. Monthly.
Science in Short Chapters. Crown 8vo, cloth extra, 7s. 6d.
A Simple Treatise on Heat. Crown 8vo, cloth limp, with Illusts., 2s. 6d.
The Chemistry of Cookery. Crown 8vo, cloth extra, 6s.

Wilson (Dr. Andrew, F.R.S.E.), Works by:
Chapters on Evolution: A Popular History of Darwinian and Allied Theories of Development. 3rd ed. Cr. 8vo, cl. ex.,with 259 Illusts., 7s. 6d.
Leaves from a Naturalist's Notebook. Post 8vo, cloth limp, 2s. 6d.
Leisure-Time Studies, chiefly Biological. Third Edit., with New Preface. Cr. 8vo, cl. ex., with Illusts.,6s.
Studies in Life and Sense. With numerous Illusts. Cr. 8vo, cl. ex., 6s.
Common Accidents, and How to Treat them. By Dr. Andrew Wilson and others. With numerous Illusts. Cr. 8vo, 1s.; cl. limp, 1s. 6d.

Winter (J. S.), Stories by:
Post 8vo, illust. bds., 2s. each.
Cavalry Life.
Regimental Legends.

Women of the Day: A Biographical Dictionary of Notable Contemporaries. By Frances Hays. Crown 8vo, cloth extra, 5s.

Wood.—Sabina: A Novel. By Lady Wood. Post 8vo, illust. bds., 2s.

Wood (H. F.)—The Passenger from Scotland Yard: A Detective Story. By H. F. Wood. Crown 8vo, cloth extra, 6s.

Words, Facts, and Phrases: A Dictionary of Curious, Quaint, and Out-of-the-Way Matters. By Eliezer Edwards. New and cheaper issue, cr. 8vo, cl. ex., 7s. 6d.; half-bound, 9s.

Wright (Thomas), Works by:
Crown 8vo, cloth extra, 7s. 6d. each.
Caricature History of the Georges. (The House of Hanover.) With 400 Pictures, Caricatures, Squibs, Broadsides, Window Pictures, &c.
History of Caricature and of the Grotesque in Art, Literature, Sculpture, and Painting. Profusely Illustrated by F.W. Fairholt,F.S.A.

Yates (Edmund), Novels by:
Post 8vo, illustrated boards, 2s. each.
Castaway. | The Forlorn Hope.
Land at Last.

NEW NOVELS.

In Exchange for a Soul. By MARY LINSKILL, Author of "The Haven under the Hill," &c. 3 Vols., cr. 8vo.

The Deemster: A Romance of the Isle of Man. By HALL CAINE, Author of "A Son of Hagar," &c. 3 vols., cr. 8vo.

Radna; or, The Great Conspiracy of 1881. By the Princess OLGA. Crown 8vo, cloth extra, 6s.

Old Blazer's Hero. By D. CHRISTIE MURRAY. Crown 8vo, cloth extra, 6s.

The Heir of Linne. By ROBERT BUCHANAN. Two Vols., crown 8vo.

Pine and Palm. By MONCURE D. CONWAY. 2 Vols., crown 8vo.

Seth's Brother's Wife. By HAROLD FREDERIC. 2 Vols., cr. 8vo.

Every Inch a Soldier. By M. J. COLQUHOUN. Three Vols., cr. 8vo.

One Traveller Returns. By D. CHRISTIE MURRAY and HENRY HERMAN. Crown 8vo, cloth, 6s.

The Passenger from Scotland Yard. By H. F. WOOD. Crown 8vo, cloth, 6s.

THE PICCADILLY NOVELS.

Popular Stories by the Best Authors. LIBRARY EDITIONS, many Illustrated, crown 8vo, cloth extra, 3s. 6d. each.

BY GRANT ALLEN.
Philistia.
In all Shades.

BY THE AUTHOR OF "JOHN HERRING."
Red Spider.

BY W. BESANT & JAMES RICE.
Ready-Money Mortiboy.
My Little Girl.
The Case of Mr. Lucraft.
This Son of Vulcan.
With Harp and Crown
The Golden Butterfly.
By Celia's Arbour.
The Monks of Thelema.
'Twas in Trafalgar's Bay.
The Seamy Side.
The Ten Years' Tenant.
The Chaplain of the Fleet.

BY WALTER BESANT.
All Sorts and Conditions of Men.
The Captains' Room.
All In a Garden Fair.
Dorothy Forster. | Uncle Jack.
Children of Gibeon.
The World Went Very Well Then.

BY ROBERT BUCHANAN.
Child of Nature.
God and the Man.
The Shadow of the Sword.
The Martyrdom of Madeline.
Love Me for Ever.
Annan Water. | The New Abelard.
Matt. | Foxglove Manor.
The Master of the Mine.

BY HALL CAINE.
The Shadow of a Crime.
A Son of Hagar.

BY MRS. H. LOVETT CAMERON.
Deceivers Ever. | Juliet's Guardian.

BY MORTIMER COLLINS.
Sweet Anne Page. | Transmigration.
From Midnight to Midnight.

MORTIMER & FRANCES COLLINS.
Blacksmith and Scholar
The Village Comedy.
You Play me False.

BY WILKIE COLLINS.
Antonina. | The Frozen Deep.
Basil. | The Law and the
Hide and Seek. | Lady.
The Dead Secret. | The Two Destinies
Queen of Hearts. | Haunted Hotel.
My Miscellanies. | The Fallen Leaves
Woman in White. | Jezebel's Daughter
The Moonstone. | The Black Robe.
Man and Wife. | Heart and Science
Poor Miss Finch. | "I Say No."
Miss or Mrs. ? | Little Novels.
New Magdalen.

BY DUTTON COOK.
Paul Foster's Daughter.

BY WILLIAM CYPLES.
Hearts of Gold.

BY ALPHONSE DAUDET.
The Evangelist; or, Port Salvation.

BY JAMES DE MILLE.
A Castle in Spain.

BY J. LEITH DERWENT.
Our Lady of Tears.
Circe's Lovers.

BY M. BETHAM-EDWARDS.
Felicia.

BY MRS. ANNIE EDWARDES.
Archie Lovell.

BY PERCY FITZGERALD.
Fatal Zero.

BY R. E. FRANCILLON.
Queen Cophetua.
One by One.
A Real Queen.
Prefaced by Sir BARTLE FRERE.
Pandurang Hari.

BY EDWARD GARRETT.
The Capel Girls.

PICCADILLY NOVELS, *continued—*

BY CHARLES GIBBON.
Robin Gray.
What will the World Say?
In Honour Bound.
Queen of the Meadow.
The Flower of the Forest.
A Heart's Problem.
The Braes of Yarrow.
The Golden Shaft.
Fancy Free.
Of High Degree.
Loving a Dream.
A Hard Knot.

BY THOMAS HARDY.
Under the Greenwood Tree.

BY JULIAN HAWTHORNE.
Garth.
Ellice Quentin.
Sebastian Strome.
Prince Saroni's Wife
Dust.
Fortune's Fool.
Beatrix Randolph.
Miss Cadogna.
Love—or a Name.

BY SIR A. HELPS.
Ivan de Biron.

BY MRS. ALFRED HUNT.
Thornicroft's Model.
The Leaden Casket.
Self-Condemned.
That other Person.

BY JEAN INGELOW.
Fated to be Free.

BY R. ASHE KING.
A Drawn Game.
"The Wearing of the Green."

BY HENRY KINGSLEY.
Number Seventeen.

BY E. LYNN LINTON.
Patricia Kemball.
Atonement of Leam Dundas.
The World Well Lost.
Under which Lord?
With a Silken Thread.
The Rebel of the Family
"My Love!" | Ione.
Paston Carew.

BY HENRY W. LUCY.
Gideon Fleyce.

BY JUSTIN McCARTHY.
The Waterdale Neighbours.
A Fair Saxon.
Dear Lady Disdain.
Miss Misanthrope.
Donna Quixote.
The Comet of a Season.
Maid of Athens.
Camiola.

BY MRS. MACDONELL.
Quaker Cousins.

PICCADILLY NOVELS, *continued—*

BY FLORENCE MARRYAT.
Open! Sesame! | Written in Fire.

BY D. CHRISTIE MURRAY.
Life's Atonement. | Coals of Fire.
Joseph's Coat. | Val Strange.
A Model Father. | Hearts.
By the Gate of the Sea
The Way of the World.
A Bit of Human Nature.
First Person Singular.
Cynic Fortune.

BY MRS. OLIPHANT.
Whiteladies.

BY MARGARET A. PAUL.
Gentle and Simple.

BY JAMES PAYN.
Lost Sir Massingberd. | From Exile.
Best of Husbands | A Grape from a Thorn.
Walter's Word. | For Cash Only.
Less Black than We're Painted. | Some Private Views.
By Proxy. | The Canon's Ward.
High Spirits.
Under One Roof. | Talk of the Town.
A Confidential Agent. | Glow-worm Tales.

BY E. C. PRICE.
Valentina. | The Foreigners.
Mrs. Lancaster's Rival.

BY CHARLES READE.
It is Never Too Late to Mend.
Hard Cash.
Peg Woffington.
Christie Johnstone.
Griffith Gaunt. | Foul Play.
The Double Marriage.
Love Me Little, Love Me Long.
The Cloister and the Hearth.
The Course of True Love.
The Autobiography of a Thief.
Put Yourself in His Place.
A Terrible Temptation.
The Wandering Heir. | A Simpleton
A Woman-Hater. | Readiana.
Singleheart and Doubleface.
The Jilt.
Good Stories of Men and other Animals.

BY MRS. J. H. RIDDELL.
Her Mother's Darling.
Prince of Wales's Garden-Party.
Weird Stories.

BY F. W. ROBINSON.
Women are Strange.
The Hands of Justice.

BY JOHN SAUNDERS.
Bound to the Wheel.
Guy Waterman.
Two Dreamers.
The Lion in the Path.

CHATTO & WINDUS, PICCADILLY. 29

PICCADILLY NOVELS, *continued*—

BY KATHARINE SAUNDERS.
Joan Merryweather.
Margaret and Elizabeth.
Gideon's Rock. | Heart Salvage.
The High Mills. | Sebastian.

BY T. W. SPEIGHT.
The Mysteries of Heron Dyke.

BY R. A. STERNDALE.
The Afghan Knife.

BY BERTHA THOMAS.
Proud Maisie. | Cressida.
The Violin-Player.

BY ANTHONY TROLLOPE.
The Way we Live Now.
Frau Frohmann. | Marion Fay.
Kept in the Dark.
Mr. Scarborough's Family.
The Land-Leaguers.

PICCADILLY NOVELS, *continued*—

BY FRANCES E. TROLLOPE.
Like Ships upon the Sea.
Anne Furness.
Mabel's Progress.

BY IVAN TURGENIEFF, &c.
Stories from Foreign Novelists.

BY SARAH TYTLER.
What She Came Through.
The Bride's Pass.
Saint Mungo's City.
Beauty and the Beast.
Noblesse Oblige.
Citoyenne Jacqueline.
The Huguenot Family.
Lady Bell.
Buried Diamonds.

BY C. C. FRASER-TYTLER.
Mistress Judith.

CHEAP EDITIONS OF POPULAR NOVELS.
Post 8vo, illustrated boards, 2s. each.

BY EDMOND ABOUT.
The Fellah.

BY HAMILTON AÏDÉ.
Carr of Carrlyon. | Confidences.

BY MRS. ALEXANDER.
Maid, Wife, or Widow?
Valerie's Fate.

BY GRANT ALLEN.
Strange Stories.
Philistia.
Babylon.

BY SHELSLEY BEAUCHAMP.
Grantley Grange.

BY W. BESANT & JAMES RICE.
Ready-Money Mortiboy.
With Harp and Crown.
This Son of Vulcan. | My Little Girl.
The Case of Mr. Lucraft.
The Golden Butterfly.
By Celia's Arbour.
The Monks of Thelema.
'Twas in Trafalgar's Bay.
The Seamy Side.
The Ten Years' Tenant.
The Chaplain of the Fleet.

BY WALTER BESANT.
All Sorts and Conditions of Men.
The Captains' Room.
All in a Garden Fair.
Dorothy Forster.
Uncle Jack.

BY FREDERICK BOYLE.
Camp Notes. | Savage Life.
Chronicles of No-man's Land.

BY BRET HARTE.
An Heiress of Red Dog.
The Luck of Roaring Camp.
Californian Stories.
Gabriel Conroy. | Flip.
Maruja. | A Phyllis of the Sierras.

BY ROBERT BUCHANAN.
The Shadow of the Sword. | The Martyrdom of Madeline.
A Child of Nature. | Annan Water.
God and the Man. | The New Abelard.
Love Me for Ever. | Matt.
Foxglove Manor.
The Master of the Mine.

BY MRS. BURNETT.
Surly Tim.

BY HALL CAINE.
The Shadow of a Crime.

BY MRS. LOVETT CAMERON.
Deceivers Ever. | Juliet's Guardian.

BY MACLAREN COBBAN.
The Cure of Souls.

BY C. ALLSTON COLLINS.
The Bar Sinister.

BY WILKIE COLLINS.
Antonina. | Queen of Hearts.
Basil. | My Miscellanies.
Hide and Seek. | Woman in White
The Dead Secret. | The Moonstone.

CHEAP POPULAR NOVELS, continued—
  WILKIE COLLINS, continued.

Man and Wife.	Haunted Hotel.
Poor Miss Finch.	The Fallen Leaves.
Miss or Mrs.?	Jezebel's Daughter
New Magdalen.	The Black Robe.
The Frozen Deep.	Heart and Science
Law and the Lady.	"I Say No."
The Two Destinies	The Evil Genius.

BY MORTIMER COLLINS.

| Sweet Anne Page. | From Midnight to |
| Transmigration. | Midnight. |

A Fight with Fortune.

MORTIMER & FRANCES COLLINS.

| Sweet and Twenty. | Frances. |

Blacksmith and Scholar.
The Village Comedy.
You Play me False.

BY DUTTON COOK.

| Leo. | Paul Foster's Daughter. |

BY C. EGBERT CRADDOCK.
The Prophet of the Great Smoky Mountains.

BY WILLIAM CYPLES.
Hearts of Gold.

BY ALPHONSE DAUDET.
The Evangelist; or, Port Salvation.

BY JAMES DE MILLE.
A Castle in Spain.

BY J. LEITH DERWENT.

| Our Lady of Tears. | Circe's Lovers. |

BY CHARLES DICKENS.

| Sketches by Boz. | Oliver Twist. |
| Pickwick Papers. | Nicholas Nickleby |

BY MRS. ANNIE EDWARDES.

| A Point of Honour. | Archie Lovell. |

BY M. BETHAM-EDWARDS.

| Felicia. | Kitty. |

BY EDWARD EGGLESTON.
Roxy.

BY PERCY FITZGERALD.

| Bella Donna. | Never Forgotten. |

The Second Mrs. Tillotson.
Polly.
Seventy-five Brooke Street.
The Lady of Brantome.

BY ALBANY DE FONBLANQUE.
Filthy Lucre.

BY R. E. FRANCILLON.

| Olympia. | Queen Cophetua. |
| One by One. | A Real Queen. |

Prefaced by Sir H. BARTLE FRERE.
Pandurang Hari.

BY HAIN FRISWELL.
One of Two

BY EDWARD GARRETT.
The Capel Girls.

CHEAP POPULAR NOVELS, continued—
  BY CHARLES GIBBON.

Robin Gray.	The Flower of the Forest.
For Lack of Gold.	
What will the World Say?	Braes of Yarrow. The Golden Shaft.
In Honour Bound.	Of High Degree.
In Love and War.	Fancy Free.
For the King.	Mead and Stream.
In Pastures Green	Loving a Dream.
Queen of the Meadow.	A Hard Knot. Heart's Delight.
A Heart's Problem	

BY WILLIAM GILBERT.
Dr. Austin's Guests.
The Wizard of the Mountain.
James Duke.

BY JAMES GREENWOOD.
Dick Temple.

BY JOHN HABBERTON.

| Brueton's Bayou. | Country Luck. |

BY ANDREW HALLIDAY.
Every-Day Papers.

BY LADY DUFFUS HARDY.
Paul Wynter's Sacrifice.

BY THOMAS HARDY.
Under the Greenwood Tree.

BY J. BERWICK HARWOOD.
The Tenth Earl.

BY JULIAN HAWTHORNE.

| Garth. | Sebastian Strome |
| Ellice Quentin. | Dust. |

Prince Saroni's Wife.

| Fortune's Fool. | Beatrix Randolph. |

BY SIR ARTHUR HELPS.
Ivan de Biron.

BY MRS. CASHEL HOEY.
The Lover's Creed.

BY TOM HOOD.
A Golden Heart.

BY MRS. GEORGE HOOPER.
The House of Raby.

BY TIGHE HOPKINS.
'Twixt Love and Duty.

BY MRS. ALFRED HUNT.
Thornicroft's Model.
The Leaden Casket.
Self-Condemned.

BY JEAN INGELOW.
Fated to be Free.

BY HARRIETT JAY.
The Dark Colleen.
The Queen of Connaught.

BY MARK KERSHAW.
Colonial Facts and Fictions.

BY R. ASHE KING.
A Drawn Game.
"The Wearing of the Green."

BY HENRY KINGSLEY.
Oakshott Castle.

BY E. LYNN LINTON.
Patricia Kemball.
The Atonement of Leam Dundas.

CHATTO & WINDUS, PICCADILLY. 31

CHEAP POPULAR NOVELS, *continued*—
E. LYNN LINTON, *continued*—
The World Well Lost.
Under which Lord ?
With a Silken Thread.
The Rebel of the Family.
"My Love." | Ione.

BY HENRY W. LUCY.
Gideon Fleyce.

BY JUSTIN McCARTHY.
Dear Lady Disdain | Miss Misanthrope
The Waterdale | Donna Quixote.
  Neighbours. | The Comet of a
My Enemy's | Season.
  Daughter. | Maid of Athens.
A Fair Saxon. | Camiola.
Linley Rochford. |

BY MRS. MACDONELL.
Quaker Cousins.

BY KATHARINE S. MACQUOID.
The Evil Eye. | Lost Rose.

BY W. H. MALLOCK.
The New Republic.

BY FLORENCE MARRYAT.
Open! Sesame | A Little Stepson.
A Harvest of Wild | Fighting the Air.
  Oats. | Written in Fire.

BY J. MASTERMAN.
Half-a-dozen Daughters.

BY BRANDER MATTHEWS.
A Secret of the Sea.

BY JEAN MIDDLEMASS.
Touch and Go. | Mr. Dorillion.

BY D. CHRISTIE MURRAY.
A Life's Atonement | Hearts.
A Model Father. | Way of the World.
Joseph's Coat. | A Bit of Human
Coals of Fire. | Nature.
By the Gate of the | First Person Sin-
  Sea. | gular.
Val Strange. | Cynic Fortune.

BY ALICE O'HANLON.
The Unforeseen.

BY MRS. OLIPHANT.
Whiteladies.

BY MRS. ROBERT O'REILLY.
Phœbe's Fortunes.

BY OUIDA.
Held in Bondage. | Two Little Wooden
Strathmore. | Shoes.
Chandos. | In a Winter City.
Under Two Flags. | Ariadne.
Idalia. | Friendship.
Cecil Castle- | Moths.
  maine's Gage. | Pipistrello.
Tricotrin. | A Village Com-
Puck. | mune.
Folle Farine. | Bimbi.
A Dog of Flanders. | Wanda.
Pascarel. | Frescoes.
Signa. [ine. | In Maremma.
Princess Naprax- | Othmar.

CHEAP POPULAR NOVELS, *continued*—
BY MARGARET AGNES PAUL.
Gentle and Simple.

BY JAMES PAYN.
Lost Sir Massing- | Like Father, Like
  berd. | Son.
A Perfect Trea- | Marine Residence.
  sure. | Married Beneath
Bentinck's Tutor. | Him.
Murphy's Master. | Mirk Abbey.
A County Family. | Not Wooed, but
At Her Mercy. | Won.
A Woman's Ven- | Less Black than
  geance. | We're Painted.
Cecil's Tryst. | By Proxy.
Clyffards of Clyffe | Under One Roof.
The Family Scape- | High Spirits.
  grace. | Carlyon's Year.
Foster Brothers. | A Confidential
Found Dead. | Agent.
Best of Husbands. | Some Private
Walter's Word. | Views.
Halves. | From Exile.
Fallen Fortunes. | A Grape from a
What He Cost Her | Thorn.
Humorous Stories | For Cash Only.
Gwendoline's Har- | Kit: A Memory.
  vest. | The Canon's Ward
£200 Reward. | Talk of the Town.

BY C. L. PIRKIS.
Lady Lovelace.

BY EDGAR A. POE.
The Mystery of Marie Roget.

BY E. C. PRICE.
Valentina. | The Foreigners.
Mrs. Lancaster's Rival.
Gerald.

BY CHARLES READE.
It Is Never Too Late to Mend.
Hard Cash. | Peg Woffington.
Christie Johnstone.
Griffith Gaunt.
Put Yourself in His Place.
The Double Marriage.
Love Me Little, Love Me Long.
Foul Play.
The Cloister and the Hearth.
The Course of True Love.
Autobiography of a Thief.
A Terrible Temptation.
The Wandering Heir.
A Simpleton. | A Woman-Hater.
Readiana. | The Jilt.
Singleheart and Doubleface.
Good Stories of Men and other
  Animals.

BY MRS. J. H. RIDDELL.
Her Mother's Darling.
Prince of Wales's Garden Party.
Weird Stories. | Fairy Water.
The Uninhabited House.
The Mystery in Palace Gardens.

BY F. W. ROBINSON.
Women are Strange.
The Hands of Justice.

BOOKS PUBLISHED BY CHATTO & WINDUS.

CHEAP POPULAR NOVELS, *continued*—
BY JAMES RUNCIMAN.
Skippers and Shellbacks.
Grace Balmaign's Sweetheart.
Schools and Scholars.
BY W. CLARK RUSSELL.
Round the Galley Fire.
On the Fo'k'sle Head.
In the Middle Watch.
BY BAYLE ST. JOHN.
A Levantine Family.
BY GEORGE AUGUSTUS SALA.
Gaslight and Daylight.
BY JOHN SAUNDERS.
Bound to the Wheel.
One Against the World.
Guy Waterman.
The Lion in the Path.
Two Dreamers.
BY KATHARINE SAUNDERS.
Joan Merryweather.
Margaret and Elizabeth.
The High Mills.
Heart Salvage. | Sebastian.
BY GEORGE R. SIMS.
Rogues and Vagabonds.
The Ring o' Bells.
Mary Jane's Memoirs.
BY ARTHUR SKETCHLEY.
A Match in the Dark.
BY T. W. SPEIGHT.
The Mysteries of Heron Dyke.
BY R. A. STERNDALE.
The Afghan Knife.
BY R. LOUIS STEVENSON.
New Arabian Nights. | Prince Otto.
BY BERTHA THOMAS.
Cressida. | Proud Maisie.
The Violin-Player.
BY W. MOY THOMAS.
A Fight for Life.
BY WALTER THORNBURY.
Tales for the Marines.
BY T. ADOLPHUS TROLLOPE.
Diamond Cut Diamond.
BY ANTHONY TROLLOPE.
The Way We Live Now.
The American Senator.
Frau Frohmann.
Marion Fay.
Kept in the Dark.
Mr. Scarborough's Family.
The Land-Leaguers.
The Golden Lion of Granpere.
John Caldigate.
By FRANCES ELEANOR TROLLOPE.
Like Ships upon the Sea.
Anne Furness. | Mabel's Progress.
BY J. T. TROWBRIDGE.
Farnell's Folly.
BY IVAN TURGENIEFF, &c.
Stories from Foreign Novelists.

CHEAP POPULAR NOVELS, *continued*—
BY MARK TWAIN.
Tom Sawyer. | A Tramp Abroad.
A Pleasure Trip on the Continent of Europe.
The Stolen White Elephant.
Huckleberry Finn.
Life on the Mississippi.
BY C. C. FRASER-TYTLER.
Mistress Judith.
BY SARAH TYTLER.
What She Came Through.
The Bride's Pass.
Saint Mungo's City.
Beauty and the Beast.
Noblesse Oblige.
Lady Bell.
BY J. S. WINTER.
Cavalry Life. | Regimental Legends.
BY LADY WOOD.
Sabina.
BY EDMUND YATES.
Castaway. | The Forlorn Hope.
Land at Last.
ANONYMOUS.
Paul Ferroll.
Why Paul Ferroll Killed his Wife.

POPULAR SHILLING BOOKS.

Jeff Briggs's Love Story. By BRET HARTE.
The Twins of Table Mountain. By BRET HARTE.
Mrs. Gainsborough's Diamonds. By JULIAN HAWTHORNE.
Kathleen Mavourneen. By Author of "That Lass o' Lowrie's."
Lindsay's Luck. By the Author of "That Lass o' Lowrie's."
Pretty Polly Pemberton. By the Author of "That Lass o' Lowrie's."
Trooping with Crows. By Mrs. PIRKIS.
The Professor's Wife. By LEONARD GRAHAM.
A Double Bond. By LINDA VILLARI.
Esther's Glove. By R. E. FRANCILLON.
The Garden that Paid the Rent. By TOM JERROLD.
Curly. By JOHN COLEMAN. Illustrated by J. C. DOLLMAN.
Beyond the Gates. By E. S. PHELPS.
Old Maid's Paradise. By E. S. PHELPS.
Burglars in Paradise. By E.S. PHELPS.
Jack the Fisherman. By E. S. PHELPS.
Doom: An Atlantic Episode. By JUSTIN H. MACCARTHY, M.P.
Our Sensation Novel. Edited by JUSTIN H. MACCARTHY, M.P.
A Barren Title. By T. W. SPEIGHT.
Wife or No Wife? By T. W. SPEIGHT.
The Golden Hoop. By T. W. SPEIGHT.
How the Poor Live. By G. R. SIMS.
A Day's Tour. By PERCY FITZGERALD.
The Silverado Squatters. By R. LOUIS STEVENSON.

www.ingramcontent.com/pod-product-compliance
Lightning Source LLC
Chambersburg PA
CBHW031928230426
43672CB00010B/1853